WORN OUT

Worn Out

How Our Clothes Cover Up
Fashion's Sins

Alyssa Hardy

THE
NEW
PRESS

NEW YORK
LONDON

Requests for permission to reproduce selections from this book should be made through our website: https://thenewpress.com/contact.

Published in the United States by The New Press, New York, 2022
Distributed by Two Rivers Distribution

ISBN 978-1-62079-694-4 (hc)
ISBN 978-1-62097-783-5 (ebook)
CIP data is available

The New Press publishes books that promote and enrich public discussion and understanding of the issues vital to our democracy and to a more equitable world. These books are made possible by the enthusiasm of our readers; the support of a committed group of donors, large and small; the collaboration of our many partners in the independent media and the not-for-profit sector; booksellers, who often hand-sell New Press books; librarians; and above all by our authors.

www.thenewpress.com

Book design and composition by Bookbright Media
This book was set in Calluna and Sofia Pro

Printed in the United States of America

10 9 8 7 6 5 4 3 2 1

To every worker who brings style into this world. And to my mother, who taught me that every woman deserves to be heard.

Contents

WORN OUT

Introduction

WHEN YOU PICKED UP THIS BOOK, YOU PROBABLY WEREN'T anticipating a love story. I want to make it clear, though, that's what this is. I will spend a lot of time telling you that fashion is a secretive and problematic industry, that its opulence is built on horrific labor and marketing practices often perpetuated by those of us who work inside it. And that's all true. At the same time, though, fashion is the glue that pulls us all together. It's the buzz that makes you feel confident when you put on your favorite pair of jeans for a night out with your friends. It's the warmth you feel when a stranger tells you they like your top. It's the pit in your stomach when you pull your late grandmother's necklace out of your jewelry box. It's the way we preserve traditions and honor our past. It's the love affair that has framed my entire adult life.

I want to start with some familiar territory: the inescapable experience lived by any human alive today, the COVID-19 pandemic. In the early weeks, after the crisis hit most major cities around the world, those of us lucky enough to be locked up inside our houses shifted our focus from the trauma on our news screens and in our social media feeds to fashion. It wasn't just me, a person whose life revolves around the industry; it was everyone. At first, those working from home embraced the switch from slacks to sweatpants, joking about dirty pajamas and tight jeans that never saw the light of day. Our jewelry remained where we'd tossed it before the world crashed around us and our high heels were stashed in the back of our closets, replaced by UGG boots and Birkenstocks. We embraced a new type of fashion normal that let go of acceptable work attire and instead prioritized our comfort when we needed it most.

There was a lot of talk about consumption, too. In the pandemic before-times, I think most people understood that we have too many clothes, and that somehow it is bad for the environment. When the future of the world felt so uncertain, it suddenly seemed silly to have all these things growing stale in our closets, and that made many of us reevaluate our previous fashion choices. Yet need versus want only went so far to curb our shopping habits. By late summer 2020, sales for sweatpants and loungewear skyrocketed by around 600 percent. Some fast fashion brands, like Boohoo and Fashion Nova, had their best profits of all time that year. What we had in our drawers for a lazy Saturday or a night alone after work was no longer cutting it every single day of our lives, so we looked for more. Matching sweatpants sets, colorful slippers, and nap dresses were marketed to us on social media shopping platforms, and we bought in.

Those without the privilege of working from home in sweatpants all day contributed to our shift in fashion too. After mask mandates took hold in April of that year, you could find a floral face mask to match your summer dress, a sporty one for your run, or even a luxury style with a recognizable logo like the Chanel double-C print. Some workers wore custom ones given to them by their employer—my dad, for example, worked at the post office warehouse and had a USPS-branded face mask he wore every day.

You know all of this, though. Because through our style choices that year, we had another collective experience inflicted on us. Fashion and style were our happy commonplace. We could joke about not knowing how to dress or share tips about mask-wearing and it was a thread we followed together while we dealt with heavier stuff individually.

But this story of a style evolution that none of us asked for, swept up into think pieces by fashion magazines, new loungewear collections by brands, and Instagram stories from influencers, did leave something out. Behind all of these sudden changes to wardrobes was a huge problem. In the garment factories, where workers had to switch their flow to make masks and sweatpants, there was a wage crisis. Many brands, particularly in the fast fashion sector, suddenly canceled full collections that they had ordered their manufacturers to produce, leaving workers with no pay for work they had already done or, in some cases, were still doing. Others were lauded as heroes when they switched production to making PPE like hospital gowns and masks (which were in desperately short supply) but weren't even providing that protection to the workers who were making them. Many of them ended up sick or dead from the virus.

In the Los Angeles Apparel factory, owned by disgraced American Apparel founder Dov Charney—I'll get to him later too—three hundred garment workers tested positive for the coronavirus in June and three died within the following weeks. The health department eventually inspected the factory and swiftly shut it down for, as a press release noted, "flagrant violations of mandatory public health infection control orders" and failure "to cooperate with DPH's investigation of a reported COVID-19 outbreak." In other factories in Los Angeles, workers were being paid a piece rate for the masks, sometimes making only 5 cents for each one, or around $180 a week for full-time work. Notably, 80 percent of these workers are women.

Around the world, garment workers who were making masks and sweatpants at similarly low rates, often even lower, were being swept up into global crisis. In Myanmar, workers who made a vast majority of the PPE Zara donated to patients and healthcare workers in Spain were on the front lines when the military staged a coup of their government. The women-led unions left work to protest the takeover and had to beg brands to continue to employ them while they did. In India, where garment work is one of the top employment opportunities, people could not afford to stay home when the crisis hit. They got sick, and many of them died.

While this may sound like a huge oversight by government

and the fashion brands, for the workers it was business as usual. Many of them never expected to be treated with compassion or dignity during this time, but they showed up and did the work anyway. It's something I wish could have been put as a disclaimer in every single mask trend story or think piece I wrote in those months. Something like: *This mask may protect you—but no guarantees for the person who made it.*

To me, the way we treated fashion during the pandemic was emblematic of how it's always been looked at, how I used to look at it. It's something for us to consume en masse, it makes us feel good, it sparkles. Its impact on people is never discussed, just hidden in plain sight, and we all willfully look away. Even when it's supposed to protect you, it might have been hurting someone else.

This feeling came to a head in late spring 2021, when mask mandates began to be lifted in the United States. One Sunday afternoon, I walked into a bodega to buy a water. It was warmer than I anticipated, and I was wearing a blazer over my T-shirt and jeans paired with heeled boots that had been sitting sad and alone in my closet for the last fourteen months. I was on my way to visit a garment factory in Midtown Manhattan with Senator Kirsten Gillibrand. (You're supposed to wear a blazer when you meet a senator, right?) The owner of the bodega still had plastic barriers up around the cash register to protect him from the customers. Taped all over it were different types of face masks: KN95s, a cloth one that read "I Love NY," along with others that had leopard or camo print, all selling for around $5. In the moment, I didn't think anything of it. By this point, the days of mask shortages were long over;

now masks were being sold everywhere from bodegas to plant shops. They were inescapable.

I headed uptown to Thirty-Ninth Street, unsurprised by how quiet it was. New York City, even this close to Times Square, was still not the same. And the Garment District . . . well, it had been hit hard. Still, there was one place in that area that was bustling, and it's where I was going. Stepping off an elevator through a cramped office lined with racks of blazers and jumpsuits, I heard the buzz of dozens of sewing machines. Women sat with their headphones on, some cutting patterns, some organizing fascinators, and most piecing together the masks we all took for granted and made into political fodder. There was something about this factory that was different from the others I was reporting on throughout the year: the workers were unionized. They made a living wage, and they knew exactly who they were making masks and clothing for. Some people I spoke with for a story I was working on were honest about the fears they had coming in to work every day, but also shared the sense of duty they felt to make masks to protect people.

"I was so scared," a woman named Chen Li said. "My mother didn't want me to go to work, I didn't want to. I wore a suit of plastic by the time I went back to make the masks." When we spoke, Chen Li was reaching the end of her mask duty and was switching over to making the samples for the Ralph Lauren Olympic uniforms. She laughed about it as she explained that the samples were really difficult after months of making simple masks. I held one of the pieces up to myself, running my hand over the embroidered American flag placed strategically on a breast pocket. Chen smiled as I did. "See!" she exclaimed. "You have to use way more of your brain to make that but I am proud of both."

As I left, I thought about how scared I was during certain parts of 2020 but how my worries were alleviated by the skilled and undervalued work of people like Chen Li. When we praised essential workers, no one talked about the people behind the sewing machines. Fashion laborers have never been seen in the light they should be. They are the pulse of this industry—not the runway strobe lights or the impossibly beautiful models, or even the expensive garments themselves, the parts that I used to think were what fashion was all about.

For me, the transition from worshipper to critic came in small increments, each one building upon a foundation of youthful adoration that eventually turned to skepticism.

During the fall of my senior year of high school, I had the flu. It was the kind of quick illness that knocks you off your feet and has you sucking on ice chips until you randomly wake up fine and ravenous three days later. That week, I spent every day on my parents' couch deliriously watching a cable station called FashionTV. It had mindless shows about makeovers and shopping, and in the middle of the night they would play full-length fashion shows. One night, I woke up in a sweaty haze as my fever broke. The television was still on and Valentino's Spring/Summer 2006 show was flashing across the screen. The models had bright red lips that matched the two bands fastened tightly to their heads; their thin bodies were draped in layers of lace and silk as they cascaded down the all-white runway. In my feverish haze, I was mesmerized.

Watching the alien-like models balance gracefully on platform stilettos sent a tingle down my spine and wrapped my whole body in a buzz that I could not shake. The feeling I had watching that show attached itself to me as though it were another limb. I printed out a photo of the show and taped it to my locker, fixating on the little details and escaping into them whenever I could.

At the time, I worked at Abercrombie Kids in my local mall. It was my first fashion job and I really hated it. I spent my breaks doing laps throughout the windowless building, passing the intense smells of pretzels and cinnamon at Auntie Anne's and dodging the sales pitch from a guy in a kiosk telling me he had the best straightener for my curly hair. Still, a mid-2000s job at the mall in upstate New York was my way into what I saw that night on the television screen.

When I graduated, I went to the only school in New York City that gave me a scholarship—not the greatest choice in retrospect, but school really didn't matter to me, Manhattan did. By the night of my eighteenth birthday I still hadn't made any friends, so I spent it alone after my shift at Urban Outfitters, smoking cigarettes and watching people walk down Second Avenue. I remembered it was Fashion Week (there were no influencers blogging about their front-row seats yet to remind me) and I was only a ten-minute walk from Bryant Park. I bought a new pack of Parliament Lights—legally, for the first time—and made my way to Fifty-Seventh Street. Before Fashion Week became the spectacle it is today, it took place inside "The Tents" in Bryant Park, which were literally just giant white event tents set up in the middle of the park. As I walked around, I was able to get just close enough that I could see the models walking in the back. It was the closest I'd ever been to the women I saw in magazines. I laughed when I realized that so much of the glamour was a façade brought out by lights and makeup. They were all just a bunch of teenagers like me.

Six years later, after several other retail jobs and a sad attempt at blogging, I got my first reporting gig. A now-defunct website I found on Craigslist asked me to go backstage at Fashion Week and write about the hairstyles. For my first show, I walked backstage at Lincoln Center, quietly praying that my name was actually on the list and that this wasn't all a scam. A woman with a headset confirmed that I did, in fact, belong there and ushered me to the hair and makeup area. I found a group of other backstage reporters and mingled near them, waiting for an opportunity to jump into their conversations. I realized that they weren't actually talking about the show, but rather how annoyed they were about being there. "I can't wait for this to be over," I heard one of them say.

Around me the models were staring blankly at their phones while frazzled makeup artists stabbed their faces with brushes and glitter. Some of them crouched in a corner, hair gelled and makeup plastered all over their faces, looking childlike in the harsh backstage lighting. A woman dressed in all black with a headset was yelling at another woman, also wearing black, who looked like she hadn't slept in a month. "Models, we need you in five!" someone screamed as a hairstylist rushed to put the finishing touches on their last model. The sense of urgency and seriousness bordered on absurdity. Photographers swarmed like a hive trying to capture the best backstage photo, hoping it would be the one that landed on top at the website or newspaper or magazine they worked for. The models looked so bored, but they snapped into a pose every time a camera was in their face.

I met one reporter backstage who I think could sense my newness, though she never actually said it. She asked me if I wanted to try and snag a seat to watch the show with her after we were done getting interviews. I didn't even know we could do that. She walked in front of me, gesturing for me to follow her. She was so confident with her bright red lipstick and chic blond bob. I had planned my outfit—a denim dress I got at a clothing swap and boots from Forever 21—for two weeks. I felt cheap and small. When we pushed open the curtain at the back of the runway and saw the seats filling up, a producer told us to sit down in a tone that startled me. She was like a teacher yelling at the class for passing notes.

I looked up from the front-row seat I had just accidentally acquired, and there was Anna Wintour, sitting like a queen, front row in her dark sunglasses, leading a court of other fashion editors seated behind and next to her. Other celebrities sat around her, seemingly unbothered by the sheer ridiculousness of it all as they posed coyly for the photographers waving at them to smile. They were dressed by the brand in a free outfit that no one except a rich person would wear. You couldn't tell by the photos that would end up in the tabloid the next day, but they looked uncomfortable. Suddenly, the lights dimmed, the music bumped, and the first model hit the catwalk. She looked so silly and young backstage, but on the runway, under the flash of countless cameras, she was striking. No longer in the corner, she was a deity, draped in fabric that she brought to life.

This was the pulse for me, the feeling that got me through the worst parts of my life. It's why I got into this business, and if you're reading this, it's probably part of why you love it too. Eventually I began writing about fashion for *Teen Vogue*, where I could talk about those buzzy shows but also the parts of the industry I didn't love. Like the pressure to be rail thin, which likely contributed to my own eating disorder, and the pervasive fatphobia and racism that existed around every corner. Readers wanted it too. So many young people with even a mild interest in style wanted to see a fashion magazine take accountability for the problems they perpetuate and change it through exposure.

In 2015, I received an email from a student that had a link to a story about Ivy Park, Beyoncé's line at Topshop. The report claimed that the clothing was being made using forced labor in Sri Lanka. After looking into it, the claims seemed newsworthy enough, especially to a young audience that I had already told to go buy the collection. So I wrote the story up in a short blog post for *Teen Vogue*. I kept it vague and I didn't have the time to do that much investigating beyond reading the small reports that were already out there. And though I received some great feedback from people who were as shocked as I was about the problems, for the most part the story was ignored.

It felt like everyone around me wanted to talk about an inclusive industry, but they only wanted to do that when it was comfortable. It was a huge wake-up call because it highlighted my own shortcomings. Why wasn't I looking further than story being presented to me, especially when I was aware of the prevalence of sweatshops in fashion?

A few years later, in late 2019, the *New York Times* released a scathing report about self-proclaimed "Faster Fast Fashion" brand Fashion Nova. In the story, reporter Natalie Kitroeff spoke to garment workers in Los Angeles who had been abused and underpaid to meet the tight deadlines for the brand's turn-around. While still denying any wrongdoing and calling it "categorically false" in their response to the story, the company added that they have seven hundred manufacturers that are required to adhere to a set of standards. "Any vendor found to not be in compliance is immediately put on a six-month probationary period. A second violation results in a suspension of all agreements with that vendor," a spokesperson said in a statement. And that was it. They got to move on, and so did the consumers. The workers, on the other hand, didn't see any justice or even acknowledgment of their experience. In 2020, Fashion Nova's profits grew.

From the runway, fashion looks like an industry full of beauty and privilege, but the factory floor tells a different story. Far from the expensive clothes and social media posts about glamorous dinners, garment workers stay hidden, sometimes bringing their own toilet paper in a lunch bag because their boss won't provide it for them. They're working as fast as they can, threading and cutting patterns to meet demand. Their hands are overworked from constantly moving them back and forth on a sewing machine, but they stay silent. There are no systems in place to protect them from abuse or manipulation.

I had to ask myself how I could write about the need for

change in fashion without examining what this meant for the industry beyond the designers and the models. Garment work is skilled work. Fashion is not frivolous. And there is so much change that we need. The first step, though, is actually talking about the problem, and that's what I'm going to do in this book. Like the clothing the garment workers make, our stories have power.

In this book, you'll learn about all of the ways that the fashion industry works to actively cover up and perpetuate climate change and labor injustice. It's a complicated Pandora's box that can be overwhelming but also liberating as an informed consumer. You will meet women who have experienced abuse, sexual assault, wage theft, and illness all within the confines of the factories that employ them to make our clothing. And you will also read stories from activists and designers who are working to change things from the inside.

This book is for anyone who has ever loved clothing and the way it can make you feel. If there is one thing I hope you take away from reading this, it's that despite its flaws, loving fashion is not the problem, it's the ways in which we consume it that can be.

1

New Arrivals

I LIVE NEXT DOOR TO A LAUNDROMAT IN QUEENS, NEW YORK. The parking lot is small but busy, with cars coming in and out, playing music and honking at each other at all times of the day. In the back of the lot, closest to my bedroom window, there is a white-and-green container with the formula "clothes + shoes = trees" in a large white font on the side. There's no further explanation to this equation. We are led to believe that somehow you end up with trees if you feed the container your old clothing and shoes. You place a bag of used stuff onto the open space in the front and pull the handle up. When you let go, it will dump whatever you're getting rid of into the back. The metal door will make a loud bang as discarded clothing lands in a sad heap of even more discarded pieces. Like most New Yorkers who learn to drown out the unique noises of their city block, I don't even notice when it happens anymore.

I'm not sure if the people putting clothing into that container know where it's going. I certainly didn't for a long time. My weak conjecture was that the tree part was a metaphor for new life, and maybe my old dresses were going to end up on a rack at Goodwill, waiting for the right person to pick them up and love them in a way that I couldn't anymore. I didn't think about it much more than that, because when I get rid of clothing, I'm usually cleansing my physical space and, more important, my mental one. I have so many clothes built on years of chasing trends and working in the fashion industry, where a perk of a low-paying journalism job is free stuff I didn't ask for. Closing that heavy handle removes those items from my world, alleviating the physical and emotional weight of a bag of unwanted clothing. I don't ever have to think about them again.

But someone else does.

Before clothing gets purchased and stashed away in our wardrobes, it had a life. A life at the hands of the person farming the cotton, the woman sewing it together, the one who packs it into a shipment, and again with the person who delivers it to our doors. If it goes into a store, it has a life with the retail worker who had to pull it out of a box and take out all of the wrinkles with a hot steamer before placing it on a hanger in a way that will catch our eye. Then it comes to live with us, where we give it energy, wearing it to parties and to work, or on dates and to dinners. We make memories with a garment that are punctuated with a small wine stain or the pull of a thread that got caught in a chair. But after it's gone out of style or worn so often that we no longer like it, we remove it from our purview, and its life goes on without us.

It would be great if our previously loved clothing landed in the closet of another person who can wear it like new and breathe life back into the fabric, but that's not always what happens. Even with the immense growth of peer-to-peer resale apps like Poshmark, Etsy, and Depop, most of the clothing people discard ends up in recycling bins like the one next door to my apartment. Chances are, those discarded clothes go into a bundle with a bunch of other clothing to be sold around the world in the multibillion-dollar international resale market.

It just as well might find its way to Sel Kofiga, a Ghanaian artist who has an intimate relationship with the way clothing is disposed. When he was young, his parents wouldn't let him shop at Ghana's thriving secondhand market because it was, as he put it, "the white man's used stuff."

And they were right. Each week 15 million items of clothing are brought into the port in Ghana to be placed in the country's thriving secondhand markets. Many of the used items that line the streets of the famous Kantamanto market in Accra, the second-largest market in the country, are from Europe and the United States, which consumes over 36 billion units of clothing each year. Eighty-five percent of those units are discarded, which is quadruple the number from just five years ago.[1]

The pieces I hear being tossed into the green bin night after night are the same ones Kofiga sees in huge, messy piles near his home. "We don't need this much," he said as he spoke about the work he does: photographing the market and using the fabrics he finds to create art pieces that bring awareness to just how much clothing exists in the world. "Trends," he told me. "They are the problem because we have more clothing than we can even wear."

Kofiga's photos highlight the mountain-like heaps of abandoned clothing that have traveled around the world and landed in his city. In one image, a few people pick through a pile of denim that is taller than a grown man standing beside it. The jeans look lifeless and dirty as one person holds them out, inspecting them to determine whether they will be suitable for resale. There is so much clothing coming into the area that, often, the heavy bundles carried by workers off of shipping containers don't even make it into the streets to be sold by vendors, and instead are placed in a warehouse to sit for years. "I have been going to these market spaces for as long as I know. It's traumatizing to be there and to know that [the bundles of clothing] are so unbelievably heavy and they are being carried by an eleven-year-old or twelve-year-old because they have to do this to earn money to send money home. It's traumatizing to go to the market spaces and see the same items of clothing just sit there for the past ten years," he said.

As Kofiga described the market, he emphasized that it is an essential part of the daily lives of the people in the city. The maze of fabric and shoes shipped in from the United States has become integral to the economy, and it is how many families make a living, but, he surmised, it shouldn't be that way. Many African countries once had thriving garment industries, but those jobs left as the secondhand markets grew. This economic structure was forced upon the countries by the overbearing power held by Europe and the United States that continues to be wielded against them.

In 2018, East African Community (EAC) members Kenya, Tanzania, Rwanda, and Uganda introduced tariffs on imported clothing in an attempt to both decrease the amount of secondhand apparel and footwear coming into their countries and grow back the local garment industry. In response, then-president Donald Trump retaliated by saying that the United States would remove any participating country's duty-free status under the African Growth and Opportunity Act if they were to participate in implementing these tariffs. In Kenya, Tanzania, and Uganda, the governments succumbed to the pressure and quickly backed down, allowing the secondhand markets to continue to grow and thrive.[2] Rwanda, however, moved forward with the tariffs and is slowly attempting to fade out secondhand imports, potentially creating huge job losses as they begin to revitalize the local garment industry.

The United States claimed that Rwanda needed to continue taking imports of secondhand clothing because otherwise it would hurt the environment and jobs in the United States. The lobbyist group Secondary Materials and Recycled Textiles pushed for the bill, arguing that thousands of pounds of clothing would end up in landfills and forty thousand jobs would be lost. In markets like the ones in Kigali, the number of garments and the warehouses filled with dirty and unsaleable textiles that come in only to sit there for years are the problem. Sometimes those items, especially the fast fashion pieces, are thrown into the aisles between seller booths to be swept up and put into a landfill because they are so broken down or unwearable they are deemed worthless.

The thousands of garments that end up in donation boxes often make a long, expensive journey to the other side of the world, only to get swept up alongside trash. There was no care for how our clothing would impact the countries it was being sent to as long as it was out of our way.

When looking at fashion from a personal perspective—thinking that you just like what you like, when you like it—it's hard to see how we are all influenced by the super-fast trend cycles. It's that feeling when you go to your closet and look at all of the clothing you have and wonder why you have nothing to wear. You might pull out a pair of pants you bought recently, holding them up and knowing you'll never put them on, but you keep them in the hope that, someday, you'll like them again. The next day you scroll through the internet and see a pair of pants that feel more trendy, more of-the-moment somehow, and so, still charged with emotions around not feeling cool enough wearing what you already have, you buy them. Fashion brands count on that emotion for sales and have twisted the idea of seasons to keep us feeling this way.

With the amount of clothing that has already been produced, there is no practical need to make new items every season, and yet the brands continue to do it for one straightforward reason: the corporations' bottom line. Garment factories that employ millions of people could focus on repairing and remaking what has already been produced instead of constantly making new pieces with virgin fabrics. However, recycling used fabric is a more expensive process than creating new plastic-based materials like nylon, organza, and faux fur and leather. Changing these methods could threaten the tried-and-true strategy of making us all feel like we need to keep up with trends to fit into society.

In the early twentieth century, luxury fashion designers showed their collections twice a year—in summer and winter—and department stores followed suit. Brands would have fashion parades inside department stores, where models would wear the latest designs and show them off to potential buyers from around the world. By the 1950s, designers were having famous women like Grace Kelly and Suzy Parker model their clothing down high catwalks as lights changed colors around them. In the sixties, as people began to look to fashion as an expression of values, the homogeneity of traditional women's clothing began to deteriorate. There was demand for more clothing and different styles. British designer Mary Quant, often touted as the designer of the miniskirt, was at the forefront of rejecting the two traditional fashion seasons of winter and summer clothes. Fashion historian James Laver explains how she was part of this shift in *Costume and Fashion: A Concise History*: "Rejecting the constraints of seasonal shows, she produced as many as twenty-eight collections during her early years, creating simple, practical, often mix n' match designs which had an element of classlessness perfectly suited to the mood of the sixties," he writes.[3]

Within a few decades, the fashion calendar had sped up to not only reflect changing tastes but to accommodate the appetites of "more seasoned jet-setters," as a 2008 *Daily Front Row* article described it. Essentially, as the wealth gap grew in the early 2000s and the rich got richer, fashion brands responded to their desire to buy more by adding Resort and Pre-Fall between the Spring/Summer and Fall/Winter seasons. Sometimes brands will also release what's called a diffusion line, like when a celebrity makes a "collection" with a major brand, or there is some sort of collaboration that will happen at a time outside of the seasonal catalog.

What comes down the runway may seem like a lofty, untouchable part of fashion, but eventually it makes its way to department stores through the careful and calculated purchases of fashion buyers. These people are the Wizard of Oz of trends. They see what the designers are making, and they decide what they think will sell to shoppers. Author Salman Rushdie once explained *The Wizard of Oz* as a film "whose driving force is the inadequacy of adults."[4] Of course, the Wizard himself is part of that analysis, but he also preys on the weaknesses of others in the film. In a similar way, our inability to distinguish between need and want when it comes to shopping trends allows brands to use those desires to sell more. One major department store buyer who asked to remain anonymous explained to me that her job is all about looking at the current social climate and predicting what her shoppers will want three to six months from now. In the last few years, this process has evolved from simple curation to searching for enough variety and quantity to keep up with the constant need for more. "I've been buying for ten years and in the last six, I have been buying so much more," she told me over the phone. "I am buying more now than ever both in depth, meaning the number of units of each style, and in breadth, meaning the offering of styles from a particular collection."

She went on to say that only a few items from the collections you see on the runway make it to the stores; it's the luxury entry point items that change only slightly from season to season that are the big sellers. For example, department stores will always keep a surplus of Gucci slides in stock, which retail for around $300, often buying new colors and styles every few months. Stores do this because people who want to buy into luxury but may not have disposable income are more likely to be able to afford those shoes instead of an outfit or a bag. As the buyer told me this, I was sitting in a Los Angeles hotel lobby, which led to a pool, and I looked out at the group of young people in front of me. Three of them had on various versions of that exact Gucci slide she was referring to. It reminded me of just how calculated it all is—those slides are a trend because they allow people to buy into something that makes them feel special. It gives the illusion of luxury, wealth, and even community. You belong to the club, and only other club members are in the know.

As a fashion editor and someone who is often invited to fashion shows in order to review them, I see an alarming number of seasonal collections. I watch catwalk after catwalk of beautiful garments cascading down the runway. I run from one fashion show to the next, talking about the trends of the season, knowing they will be usurped by other trends in only three months' time. It's the part of my job that, even though it's fun, often feels fake and kind of ridiculous. There is so much opulence and theater around new clothing that it's hard to remember why you're even there. Is it for the celebrity sitting front row getting interviewed, even though they had nothing to do with any of it? Maybe it's for the model working seventeen-hour days hoping for their big break. Could it be for editors and journalists like me, indulging in a self-serving month of being seen by industry elite and then going out to dinner to talk shit? With each passing season, I've realized that as much as I love the artistry, I was part of a machine that has lost its way. In a lot of ways, it appears that Fashion Week is there to tell us that we need new stuff all the time to keep up. In the end, though, it's the brands that make more money, and we have a bunch of clothes we don't wear.

The fashion industry has consistently proven its unwillingness to prioritize people over their own profits, and that was even more apparent to me during the fall of 2020, when the COVID-19 pandemic was about to reach its second peak in New York. Dozens of designers weren't able to afford to make a new collection of clothing for the upcoming season. The market had downshifted fast, department stores were closing and not buying as much, and customers were not looking to purchase expensive clothing when they didn't even know how or when the world would reopen again. Several brands, like Versace, Brandon Maxwell, Ralph Lauren, and Tom Ford, decided to move away from the traditional fashion calendar and make a collection in a time when they felt their customers could buy clothing again. The change was twofold, though. For a few months, it seemed like maybe these designers would be at the forefront of change, leading a shift toward the idea that we don't need new clothing or trends every season. I thought, naively, that maybe we had reached a point so far gone in late-stage capitalism that we would have to boomerang back to less. Maybe the brands would realize that adhering to an ever-growing seasonal calendar was antiquated and collectively the industry would adjust.

I was hopeful that the luxury fashion market would see how harmful the expectations to produce multiple times a year had become and do it less. But the fashion industry is not about practicality or safety for the people who work in it; it's about money. My wishful thinking was soon met with invites for virtual fashion shows, with dozens of brands opting to "meet the moment" with fashion. It was going to take so much more than a few months of global chaos to shut it down.

By early 2021, most brands were seeing their customers come back, which meant they were going to stay and continue the cycle like nothing had ever happened.

I learned from the department store buyer that after the summer of 2020, when people working from home saved money on gas and going out, the business grew. Brands jumped on the opportunity to sell to people who were looking at fashion as an escape and were eager to contribute even more to the cycle. Brands also doubled down and began producing those entry items in large quantities, knowing that people wanted to spend.

This return to overproduction impacts the entire market, not just the people who care about high fashion. The way the seasons have ramped up in luxury directly correlates to how much is getting created down market. In fast fashion there are fifty-two "micro-seasons" in the calendar based on trends we see at the higher-end brands. Yes, that means new clothes for *every single week of the year* from brands like Zara, Fashion Nova, H&M, Shein, and Boohoo. These brands analyze trends from the runway, which get amplified by celebrities and influencers, in order to design and produce them within weeks. So, while creators of the trend may take several months to put it into production, fast fashion has it ready for sale before most customers even know they want it.

"We produce clothing as the seasons happen," garment worker Santa Puac explained to me one blazing hot evening. She and I met at the Garment Worker Center in downtown Los Angeles, where she is a worker leader who advocates on behalf of her peers. She has been in the garment industry for well over a decade. When we sat down that day, she had her three children with her. Santa had just started back at work because when her daughter was born in early 2020, she was afraid her compromised immune system would make her more susceptible to catching the virus. Working in a cramped, dirty factory with little to no ventilation would be dangerous, and she said she knew plenty of workers who had died the year before.

In the spring of 2021, when cases began to decrease in Los Angeles, Santa decided to go back to work at a factory that makes Fashion Nova clothing where she was paid 5 cents per piece, at around $4 to $6 an hour, adding tags and labels to clothing that retail for up to $50. Santa confirmed that new collections are produced every week in the factory that employs her, but added that they are busier than ever because, since the pandemic started, they make masks on top of the clothes. She's working sixty hours a week just to keep up.

As a shopper, you may not realize how rapidly things are changing because it's only a rack here and there, or a few "new arrivals" on the store website per week. Sometimes the style changes are so quiet and subtle—like a different pattern on the same style of pants or a slightly altered graphic on a T-shirt— that most people don't notice. Unlike luxury, fast fashion brands are producing more because they are selling more, and they can get instant feedback through sales about what needs to change. "In the winter we are making pants and sweaters and in the summer it's bathing suits and skirts. Then they sell them right away," Santa said. "Sometimes it's just a small change."

I have seen how this works firsthand, too. When I was a teen-ager, I worked at Urban Outfitters in Midtown Manhattan. I was new to the city and everything felt so big and important, especially my minimum-wage retail job. Once a month I would have to work an overnight shift re-merchandising the entire floor along with each staff member in their various sections. Once we locked the doors, the sound of boxes being torn open and broken down by the minute would fill the floor, replacing the voices of hundreds of customers clamoring for a new pseudo-bohemian top. The music went from the generic store playlist to whatever the store manager decided they wanted to listen to.

Old merchandise would be pulled off the shelves and put into another pile ready to be marked down for sale. They would then get replaced by something similar but in a different color or size. On the men's floor there was a giant wall of graphic T-shirts. They were all the same cut and weight, they just had different images on them. The switch wasn't about replacing top sellers, it was a cycle of newness to keep customers shopping. And it worked. There were so many customers I would see once or twice a week; some would come in just to have a place with air-conditioning to hang out, and others picked up a new T-shirt every single time they came in. One man, who was famous but would hide his face in vain behind a pair of sunglasses, would ask me, "What's new?" when I saw him at the beginning of every month.

It didn't even feel unusual because, honestly, I had similar shopping habits; fast fashion and I grew up together. Forever 21 and H&M were always around, changing with the cultural patterns as I did. They allowed me to be in touch with the trends I wanted to emulate in a way that didn't feel risky—a $5 top was an hour of work at the restaurant where I answered phones in high school. Even for friends in better financial situations, it was the same thing—these stores were just where you shopped, and every Friday there was going to be something new to look at.

As I headed into a career in fashion outside of the retail floor, my shopping habits didn't change that much. While I understood overconsumption, I still overconsumed. Shopping would happen so quickly, without much thought, and the next thing I knew I had a shirt in my closet that I didn't even like that much. Often I shopped because of a feeling of insecurity. Before an interview or a work event, I would look in my closet and nothing was acceptable, everything was too outdated or not cool enough and that's when the panic would kick in. Zara was five blocks away from the office I worked in and I could get there and change in the dressing room if I walked fast enough. I would buy dresses or tops to go with pants I already had on. Taller heels, or sometimes a nicer bag would ring up a bill of just under $50. I would show up to the event and still feel under-dressed or not myself. All of these items meant nothing more than a minor fix of newness to get me through the next few hours. It was not something I was particularly proud of, mainly because I knew better. Still, even people who understand the worst parts of the fast fashion industry are not immune to its seasonal pull. We are all trained to want new, better, and more. And if you're someone who can't justify spending your money on something over $100, well, Forever 21 and H&M and Zara are going to be right there to catch you when you fall, because that's what they are made to do.

In 1985, a man named Amancio Ortega Gaona decided he wanted to change the way people shopped. That year, he founded the Inditex Group, a holding company that Zara, the brand he started in his hometown in Spain, would operate under. While other fast fashion brands like Forever 21 and

H&M had existed long before, he wanted to make clothing that was even faster. To do this, he had to revolutionize the distribution model so that Zara had more control over the entire business, from design to production to retail. The result was clothing that could replicate trends coming from the larger fashion industry, and then adjust and respond to customer feedback by changing the styles they offer week by week.

Each year Zara brings at least twelve thousand styles to market, which ship twice a week from warehouses into the stores.[5] They make enough items that anything you could ever imagine searching for is available, fresh, and new. The entire ethos is that clothing is disposable. Nothing is meant to last. "We were switching inventory out almost every day. Items either sold out so fast we needed to replace them, or some items did not sell at all. So, we got rid of them," said a former manager from one of the brand's highest-trafficked stores in the United States. "We also had two scheduled shipments per week with roughly 1,700 items per shipment for all three departments: women, men, and kids. At larger stores, they would get almost 5,000 to 6,000 units per shipment," he explained, remarking that half of that shipment was for replenishment of items sold out, and the other half was brand-new items. Of course, just like when I worked at Urban Outfitters, there isn't space to keep adding 3,000 units each week, so in order to make room, the sales associates pack and ship the low-selling items back to a warehouse, where they will eventually get marked down for sale online.

This cycle teaches us that every winter we should get a new sweater or a new jacket and that each year a new trend would leave last year's jeans in the dust. If it's on sale, even better. It makes no sense. As a kid, my mother kept a big plastic container in the bottom of my bedroom closet. Each season she and I would rotate what was on the hangers together, setting aside what no longer fit. What was previously in the box would be transferred to the hangers above. This is probably a familiar routine for anyone who grew up with changing seasons. At the beginning of fall, you pull out your favorite sweater and settle into its familiar softness. In the spring, after months of frigid temperatures, you let your arms finally feel the sun when you trade your sweatshirt for a T-shirt. When did we decide that this wasn't enough for us?

From the factory floor to the retail floor, this unnecessary cycle has hurt workers immensely. "We go out in the morning and we leave at sunset. We don't see the sun," Maria, another garment worker who made clothing for Fashion Nova, explained. "There is so much work to do, and we get paid by each item of clothing. We can't stop." Her bosses would sometimes tell her to clock out if the work wasn't done and then go back to her station and finish it before leaving for the day, unpaid for the work she was doing to fulfill the orders.

Once those orders come into the stores, the labor issues don't stop. "Full-time salary employees consistently worked overtime, especially during inventory, and were never compensated for it. Not all managers did this, but we did have managers that would tell hourly associates to clock out and continue working if a task was not complete," the former manager of Zara explained. This means that to get all of the products onto the shelves, some retail employees were working less than their hourly rate due to fear of termination. It was not surprising, then, when in 2020 a reporter for *Buzzfeed* uncovered evidence that garment workers, who are flagrantly taken advantage of, were putting in eleven-hour days and making as little as $3.75 a day to keep up with the changing shifts in business strategy during the pandemic.

Understanding the seasons in fashion is the key to grasping everything you've ever heard about the fashion industry. Landfills and sweatshops exist in tandem with the industry's relentless pursuit to have us consume more than ever before. Trends are spinning so fast, perpetuated by what we see on social media, that one generation doesn't even have time to process the style cues from their youth before a cultural reset brings them back. What's often portrayed in headlines as a culture war is a purposeful marketing tactic by the fashion industry.

Suppose Y2K didn't come back around again just a few years after those items got circulated out of your wardrobe. In that case, people growing into more disposable income wouldn't find themselves browsing online for a halter top less than a decade after their last one went into the trash. "People need to understand that no matter what it is, no matter how they are going to wear it, no matter how they're going to put it on, it is going to have an impact on somebody else's space in some time to come," Sel Kofiga said to me sternly on that call regarding the piles of clothing he sees discarded in Ghana. He recognizes that it's on the brands to stop producing and wants people to feel empowered to love their clothes and not give in to this corporate push for us to keep buying into trends literally every weekly season.

We also need to look at how much social media dictates the acceleration of production cycles and contributes to our consumption habits. On TikTok specifically, seasonal "haul" videos hosted by people shopping a newer, cheaper generation of fast fashion brands like Shein and Fashion Nova are some of the most viewed content on the platform. The idea of a haul was popularized on YouTube in the early 2010s by content creators highlighting large fast fashion shopping trips. Around 2015, the trend tapered off as vloggers grew their audiences and priorities around monetizing changed. With TikTok, a new audience evolved the idea into shorter videos with even cheaper items. During the back-to-school shopping season in the summer of 2021, there were over 3 billion views on Shein hauls. Some of the videos show people announcing the amount they spent for a "fall haul" (usually around $500) and then showing off a box filled with new items. In one popular video, the creator rates each piece from 1 to 10 and says whether or not she's going to keep it. "7.5 out of 10, it's cute but I hate the material," the caption reads as she looks into the camera with a sad face. She tugs at a stretchy pink dress that cost her $11 and shrugs. She doesn't say it, but I'd guess she's going to throw that dress into a giveaway pile that will eventually be transferred into another pile, away from the perfectly thought-out lighting of a viral video. Sure, her wallet may not feel the impact of that discarded minidress, but the person who made it and the person who might have to deal with its aftermath will.

It's not just the Sheins of the world that are part of these brazen displays of disposable consumerism. Trying to solve our fast fashion problem by thrifting might not be all that much better.

On the sustainable side of fashion TikTok, "thrift-hauls" reign supreme. In one video, a creator fills up a shopping cart with $180 worth of goods at a consignment shop. They hold up each piece before they throw it into the pile until it's overflowing with fabric. In another viral video, a fashion influencer holds up three garbage bags as they walk into their apartment. They move their hips from side to side as the video scrolls through twelve new outfits they just purchased.

While secondhand is better than buying new garments, it's the idea that we always need new clothing that keeps these fashion cycles spinning. Experts believe that by 2030, 17 percent of every person's wardrobe will be secondhand clothing bought through apps like thredUP and the RealReal.[6] Even the buyers looking at new clothes every season recognize this as the reality and plan to adjust the business model to fit the trend. "If you notice, a lot of department stores are trying to partner with resellers because they realize this is something that's not going away, we can't avoid it. So, there needs to be a way that we can then control it," the department store buyer explained. She went on to say that the idea of the buzzy fashion sustainability practice known as circularity—where clothing and accessories are designed to be regenerative and are often repurchased by the brand that created them—could be huge for luxury goods. Even with an ethical spin, which is better than making everything new all the time, the motive is always to make more money and create new things. We are all a part of this cycle that the brands designed to keep us consuming— and overlooking the consequences.

The bottom line is that we want too much at a cost that feels low but is expensive in other ways. It doesn't matter if it's thrifted or if it's brand new: buying more every season—whether it's based on the weather or the week—is what keeps the mountains of discarded clothing growing all over the world. And the people making those items continue to be exploited in ways that fashion executives don't want you to see.

2

Made in America

In Los Angeles's fashion district, mannequins line the long narrow sidewalks. Some of them are just impossibly thin legs with big fiberglass butts and wide hips showing off shapewear or stretchy denim. Others stand six feet tall with hot pink heads and DD-sized chests. You can buy a bra at the same place you could find a suit and a First Communion dress. Most of the two-mile-long area, right in the heart of the city, is similar to an East Coast boardwalk at the peak of the summer season, or a midwestern carnival in late fall. Mariachi music plays from inside one storefront while Taylor Swift blasts from another. People stand on their tippy-toes just to see past the thick and slow-moving crowd in front of them.

It smells like a mix of spices you can't place from all of the competing food carts and sandwich shops. A whiff of falafel is quickly overpowered by the distinct smell of a bacon cheeseburger. In the heat of the afternoon, though, it's the women selling freshly cut fruit under colorful umbrellas who have the longest lines. There is also signage everywhere. Red flags boosting sales of 90 percent off compete with neon signs and racks of dresses for $3.99 each. A woman who is pushing a stroller bumps into a man pushing a shaved ice cart. Even in Los Angeles, where cars are king and walking from one store to another is virtually unheard of, the streets are buzzing with people on foot.

But this district isn't just about shopping for a deeply discounted wardrobe or spending an afternoon trying different foods. It's where business happens for hundreds of retailers like Fashion Nova, Forever 21, Mango, and more. For the last twenty-five years, it's where a garment worker named Maria has been making a living.

Maria was born and raised in Mexico by her mother and father. Her parents both worked in textile factories there; the only career she's ever known is one behind a sewing machine. When she started working in 1997, it was the height of a rare transformation in the United States. While most manufacturing in every other industry had already moved production to Asia and South America, the garment industry in the United States grew so much that it was one of the top employers for people migrating to the West Coast of the United States. Work in these factories accounted for 6 percent of all jobs in the city, and people from South and Central America filled 97 percent of those jobs; 70 percent of them were women.

Los Angeles wasn't some sort of employment utopia, though. Jobs in those factories came with a heavy price. The cruel reality of garment work in the city was that the pay was extremely low, conditions were often dangerous, and the management was exploitative. And for many years, this was hidden from the mainstream view of fashion in the United States, obscured by a nationalist sentiment that U.S.-made products were somehow better than those produced abroad.

In the garment industry, things had changed too drastically over the last several decades for that to be true. In the 1930s, garment workers organized in Los Angeles and unionized with the International Ladies Garment Workers Union (ILGWU), a union formed in New York City following the Triangle Shirtwaist Factory fire. The effort was led by a labor activist and anarchist named Rose Pesotta. Pesotta was born in Derazhnya, Russia—now Ukraine—and moved to New York City in 1917. She got a job as a shirtwaist maker in Manhattan and joined the Local 25 ILGWU. Shirtwaists were a popular type of women's blouse in the early twentieth century; they were functional and modeled on men's shirts. They were also affordable and often made in sweatshops, essentially an early form of fast fashion. In 1939, after she began organizing garment workers around the country, including in Massachusetts, a *Boston Globe* article described Pesotta as a "comely miss whose figure and appearance belie her 43 years." They also said she was a "firecracker who knows her rights and stands for them."

When she got to Los Angeles, she began by organizing Mexican and Chinese immigrants working in sweatshops, and eventually she established the Local 266. She wasn't there long after, however, because she was passed up for a promotion that was given to a man. When she resigned in 1941, she wrote a letter describing the workers of Los Angeles:

> These workers—practically all women—are in the main Americans of old stock, whose forebears have been in this country for generations, many of them are former Dust Bowlers, strong characters like Ma Joad and the other Okies now situated on the Pacific Coast. They have courage and native intelligence. They read our press, look upon it seriously and know their rights under both the United States Constitution and the Constitution of the ILGWU.

She was right. In particular, the Ma Joad reference from *The Grapes of Wrath* was an apt comparison. Literary scholar Susan Shillinglaw describes Ma Joad in the *Washington Post* as "a feminist—feisty, strong, loving, resilient—and the kind of leader, then and now, who might guide the nation's jalopy through difficult times."[1] Exactly what I imagine these garment workers to be.

The contracts between the workers and the factories were upheld for several years following Pesotta's departure from the union, but by the 1970s the world had changed. The ability to import clothing from factories around the globe that were using cheap labor had made it so that factories in Los Angeles could not compete. They broke their contracts and started hiring nonunion, mostly immigrant labor. It wasn't illegal to do this and they were able to take advantage of the fact that many of the workers would not organize again for fear of deportation or retribution. By the 1990s, a "Made in the USA" label was nothing more than an empty symbol of a bygone standard, and sweatshops were rampant across Los Angeles.

In 1995, a raid on an apartment complex in El Monte, a suburb of Los Angeles, found seventy-two Thai immigrants held against their will, sleeping in the same place where they were working, making only $2 an hour. "Please be careful," a letter handwritten in pencil and delivered to authorities by the boyfriend of a woman who escaped read. "Very dangerous. Please bring much manpower." It included a map of the apartment. The letter now sits in the Smithsonian collection at the National Museum of American History.[2]

Some of these garment workers were subject to debt bondage and forced to pay back the cost of their transport to the United States out of the already low wages they made. They were not compensated at all as a result. When authorities found the makeshift factory, many of the people held captive revealed that they hadn't been allowed to leave for several years. It was one of the worst examples of the abuse workers were forced to endure throughout the city. It exposed the disparities between the fashion industry the public could see, filled with glamorous supermodels, and the one that actually existed in the '90s. As the industry elite sat front row at fashion shows in New York City, nodding as Kate Moss modeled a tan two-piece suit, there were people on the other side of the country held captive to make clothing. Those workers weren't the image that the larger American fashion industry wanted to put forth, so those at the helm of this multi-billion dollar industry stayed silent.

Thankfully, for others outside of fashion, the discovery of the El Monte sweatshop was the start of an awakening and the first baby step on a long, still-winding road. AB-633, a bill put forth by the state assembly of California and eventually signed into law in 1999, allowed workers to receive backpay for lost wages "by the failure of a garment *manufacturer, jobber, contractor, or subcontractor* to pay wages or benefits." The problem was that this bill left out the brands, and because of this, in the decades after its passage brands could continue to look the other way, as factories paid lower and lower wages. But the fantasy of American exceptionalism in fashion had cracked, and a clear line between the predatory fashion executives and the laborers had been drawn.

About two years after the El Monte factory raids, amid heightened awareness around sweatshops in the United States, another Los Angeles–made brand, Guess Inc., brought in $515 million in revenue. The five top executives made around

$12 million a year.[3] Maria and her colleagues were making $300 a week in factories just a few miles from company headquarters. And it wasn't just the executives at Guess that were getting paid top dollar at the expense of the low-paid workers. This was the golden age of supermodel-driven ad campaigns, and that year Guess spent $19 million on them. A four-page spread in *Vogue* featured Laetitia Casta, a famous "GUESS? Girl," and Victoria's Secret angel. In one image, her hair is tousled as she sits looking up at the camera, her slip dress just short enough to show the tops of her thighs. In another, she leans up against a fence, her jeans unbuttoned, revealing just a small bit of the waistband on her underwear.

There was Baby Guess, too. Those ads featured model Gigi Hadid twenty years before her big break. In that campaign, a two-year-old Hadid wears a bandana over her long blond pigtails as she looks into the camera. She's wearing a little denim jacket and a T-shirt with the brand logo on it, an image that would eventually get shared in every magazine as her career blossomed. It was notable in other ways because the black-and-white images from the '90s Guess campaigns became iconic. The images of adults sold a story of sex appeal, while the children, who were often beautiful celebrity babies, gave the brand its wholesome and attainable edge. It was gobbled up by the fashion industry as the brand bought ad spreads in magazines of up to four pages. This Los Angeles–made, all-American brand that could make you look hot in a pair of jeans and a baby tee could also make your kid look adorable in a matching jumper and jacket set.

But behind those photos was something more sinister.

In the summer of 1997, Guess also placed a peculiar advertisement in the *New York Times* and the *Washington Post*, claiming that the clothing was "guaranteed 100% free of sweatshop labor." The Department of Labor immediately refuted the ad after investigators discovered that despite the brand's claims that they were closely regulating their factories, a contractor was making workers like Maria take their work home to finish it. Because they were getting paid per garment made instead of per hour, they worked without pay. "Sometimes the boss comes up and says, 'Don't tell the Guess inspectors that I punched in the timecards for you,'" a worker claimed in a 1997 interview with the *New York Times*.[4] Guess's retort was obtuse. They claimed that the contractor using sweatshop labor was never approved, deflecting the responsibility away from the brand and onto the supply chain problems as a whole. The California labor commissioner condemned the advertisement and told the *Los Angeles Times*, "What's to stop a contractor from lying to them again?"

The scandal helped to create subtle awareness about the myth that U.S. manufacturing was better for workers. Stories of garments made by people working in unsafe conditions for fourteen hours a day made their way loudly into music and across college campuses. In 1999, Rage Against the Machine's *The Battle of Los Angeles* album went double platinum and won a Grammy Award. The band released a video for their single "Guerilla Radio," which featured garment workers in a sweatshop. The video juxtaposed this image with a parody of a Gap ad. A beautiful blond woman tries on clothing, throws down an American Express card, and strolls down the street

in high heels carrying her shopping bag. Then it cuts to workers not lifting their heads up as they work fast behind sewing
machines.

Jo-Ann Mort, then the director of communications for the
Union of Needletrades, Industrial and Textile Employees told
the *Washington Post* in 1999 that the video was working.[5] "Since
their CD came out, we've been inundated with e-mails from
young people interested in making sure the clothes they're
buying are sweatshop-free and wanting to know how they
can get involved in the Stop Sweatshops campaign," she said.
"What a band as well-known as Rage Against the Machine can
do, and is doing, is alert a younger generation, and probably the
prime consumer generation, to this issue. In our case, the link
between consumers and workers is very important."

Between 1999 and 2001, a group known as the United Students Against Sweatshops organized thousands of students
at schools ranging from Yale to the University of Kentucky
to Purdue to protest their schools for using sweatshop labor
to make merchandise. Many of these schools had previously
made licensing deals with Nike, Gear, Champion, and Fruit
of the Loom to make merchandise. All of those brands were
found to have used sweatshop labor in the mid-'90s. Students
occupied the administration buildings to pressure the institutions to adopt anti-sweatshop policies for their items.

This mobilization led to some changes on campus. Many
institutions made an effort to source items made with union
labor, and others agreed to disclose the factories they were
working with and require them to pay living wages. On a larger
scale, though, the movement lost steam. Brands were still play-

ing into people's most consumerist instincts, ignoring the few thousands of students making noise and targeting the hundreds of thousands looking for new, trendy, cheap clothing.

Forever 21, for example, was just hitting its stride. The brand was founded in Los Angeles because the founder, Do Won Chang, thought that people with the nicest cars in the city were "in the garment business." He understood that there was money to be made. In the early 2000s, the company made over $4 billion in annual sales using the micro-season model and subcontracting with factories in L.A. that paid low wages. The Forever 21 store was a regular feature at every single mall in America and around the world—and, full disclosure, its clothes were a regular feature in my closet for most of my teens and early twenties.

The brand began making new collections every three weeks at a significantly lower price than their predecessors like Gap and Guess. A pair of denim capri pants from Forever 21 cost about $27.80 in 2003, while a similar pair from Guess cost around $50. Of course, the faster, cheaper collections of clothing came with even worse conditions for workers. In 2001, nineteen garment workers sued Forever 21, alleging that they had been working twelve-hour days in horrific conditions with no overtime. Activist and immigrant labor rights professor Victor Narro helped the garment workers distribute flyers raising awareness about the situation.

> BOYCOTT Forever 21!! We are 19 garment workers who sewed Forever 21 clothes in factories in downtown Los Angeles without the guarantee of overtime

or minimum wage. We worked 10-12 hours a day, in dirty, unsafe factories. We are owed hundreds of thousands of dollars! We asked Forever 21 to take responsibility—pay us and ensure all the factories it uses follow the laws and treat the workers with respect. So far they have refused! Yet Forever 21 will make $400 million in sales! *During this holiday season help us tell Forever 21 to pay us* . . . Call Forever 21 at 213 747-2121—tell them to take responsibility! And join us here at the Highland Park store every Saturday at 3 pm until Christmas.

The company later served Narro with what is known as a SLAPP, a "strategic lawsuit against public participation." It's a well-known intimidation tactic used by corporations to silence detractors by burdening them with legal fees. In the end, the organizers and Forever 21 settled for an undisclosed amount.

On a phone call one summer afternoon, Narro told me that the defamation lawsuit intended to intimidate workers fighting for better pay, but it did not silence them. It certainly slowed down protests when lawyers were involved in legal matters, but it highlighted the important combination of worker-led and community-led organizations. The movement against Forever 21 was the first instance where people in the United States heard stories directly from the people impacted by sweatshops themselves. Consequently, the brands' reputation for using low-wage work never truly went away. There was a new understanding among shoppers about the labor used to make clothing, and it did enough damage to Forever 21's reputation to make space for another brand with an entirely different message. American Apparel, founded by Dov Charney, moved its headquarters and manufacturing to Los Angeles in 1997, where the garment district was flourishing. Six years later, the brand made the transition from wholesaling T-shirts to creating trendy hipster staples and soon became a cultural touchstone.

In 2007, I was one of the hundreds of other teenagers who moved to New York City and got a job at American Apparel. The brand's brightly colored leggings and tri-blend T-shirts defined a moment in culture. You could not walk down a street without seeing a girl wearing a headband over her forehead or a guy with a super-deep V-neck shirt. Beyoncé even came into the store once to pick up twenty pairs of leggings and a couple of bodysuits. Working there was a rite of passage.

The brand touted a vertically integrated production process, meaning that a company owns part of its production. In American Apparel's case, the company owns the factory that makes its clothing instead of contracting the work out. It's not uncommon in fast fashion (Shein and Zara are also vertically integrated), but Charney used it to highlight supply chain control. There was even a diagram of how production worked, and pictures of factory workers were taped to the registers as I rang up everyone from the broke college kid down the street to Edward Norton.

One of the qualities that made American Apparel so universally popular was that Charney loved to position activism through sex. His provocative advertisements sprawled all over

major cities, displaying young girls bent over wearing leggings or leg warmers and nothing else. Some of them would
have little messages that read "Sweatshop free" and "American
Apparel is capitalism—working."

In the spring of 2007, when I was working as a sales associ-
ate at the store in Tribeca, Charney decided to launch a campaign called "Legalize LA," which he labeled an alternative to
lobbying. The idea was to legalize all of the immigrants living in the city. While the campaign didn't do much in terms
of actual policy changes, it did bring attention to the brand.
In 2008, during the height of attention on the campaign, the
federal government appeared to escalate raids on businesses,
like American Apparel, that were known to hire immigrants.
Then-California assembly speaker Fabian Núñez stood in
front of the downtown factory and called the raids an "over-
board meat-ax approach," accusing ICE of pushing business
out of California. It highlighted how discriminatory the practice of raiding and threatening workers in factories was—there
was no indication that people working there had been doing
so illegally. Núñez called it "individualized suspicion, often
strictly based on a person's appearance."

I wore that shirt proudly—I still do. Until that point, working
in the mall in my hometown buying a shirt on a whim, I hadn't
fully grasped what sweatshops meant. But now I worked for a
company fighting fire with fire. It gave me the same clothes I
wanted, at low-ish prices, and I could feel good about it.

But that wasn't all that American Apparel was. Those same
ads that touted a sweatshop-free work environment featured
images of some American Apparel retail employees who had

been sexually harassed or assaulted. To even get the job, I had to have my photo taken in a back office by a sixteen-year-old who judged whether I was cool enough. I waited in a line that wrapped around Houston Street, dressed in red high-waisted biker shorts and a cut-up T-shirt. Everyone around me was dressed in the same sort of hipster cosplay as we waited to be called into the back room for a photo.

"Give me bed eyes," I remember the person saying with a laugh as they snapped my photo, which would later hang on a corkboard in the back.

Drugs and alcohol were all but encouraged on the retail floor. One time I walked into the staff bathroom only to find three lines of cocaine on the back of the toilet. Someone had put them there for everyone to try if they wanted to. Employees would come to work their shifts after a full night out, still drunk, and leave for the day without remembering what had happened. We would play loud music, pretend to finger-space racks, and get yelled out by Charney over a loudspeaker every once in a while. Sometimes he would sit in his office in L.A. and watch on security cameras, chiming in with demands to move racks or stand somewhere different. We would be offered products and told we could only take them if we wore them on the store floor, so sometimes that meant a zipper-front bodysuit. It didn't matter if you were uncomfortable because it was a free top, and Dov was telling you it looked good.

It all felt kind of gross. Making supply chain education a part of the business model was an incredible shift, but it was small and too easily taken at face value. Being anti-sweatshop was just as much about optics as it was any sort of social justice.

His fight against unfair labor only extended to the amount of money he was paying the people who worked for him. "Capitalism working" meant he could pay you a little more than the low average wage, and you had to shut up and take the other crap that came your way. For the factory workers, it was a secure job that was constantly jeopardized by the careless and cruel antics of the company's founder, and for the retail workers, it was sexual harassment and safety issues. Eventually, Dov Charney's behavior and sexual assault allegations caught up to him. The company ousted him in 2014, but by that time, it was too late. Just three years later, the brand shut down all its stores and sold all of its assets to Gildan, and 2,400 workers were laid off.

Four years later, Charney came back with Los Angeles Apparel, a brand similar to American Apparel, from the styles of the clothing to the marketing, that again boasted above-minimum wage for garment workers. In the beginning, with social media making the plight of garment workers more visible than ever, it seemed like consumers were willing to look past his other abuse allegations in order to support a transparent brand. True to form, though, not everything was as it seemed. In 2020, the factory was shut down after three hundred garment workers tested positive for COVID-19. Though Charney disputed any wrongdoing, health investigators found that workers were spaced using cardboard instead of plastic, which was recommended for optimal protection, and the guidelines were not translated into Spanish. Workers in the area, like Santa Puac, were so concerned about this specific outbreak that they actively turned down jobs at the factory (which does pay significantly more than others in the area) because they feared for their health and safety. "I was getting referred by friends because there was a lot of work there," she explained. "No way. I have children and I didn't want them to get sick."

Maria also had these concerns, but explained that the reason some workers ignored safety concerns was because the pay at the American Apparel factory was significantly better than what was offered in other factories. For example, she hadn't had a wage increase at her own workplace in over a decade.

Despite minimum wage increasing by around $10 and the cost of living quadrupling, she said she has had to fight for pennies. The bosses tell her it's because brands want to keep the prices low in order to compete with other manufacturers. The brands, they tell her, will just go with the cheapest option. "I complained over my pay with one employer. I even fought over half a penny," Maria told me over the phone. She let out a telling sigh. "I asked the employer like how . . . how can you pay me half a penny for my work?"

The answer she received lacked any sympathy or legality.

"When you complain, they let you know that there are other workers that are willing to take the same job you're doing for maybe cheaper. In one specific experience, I worked close to my house because my kids were little. I had to stay close to their school, so I could pick them up at the after-school program. I didn't have money to pay for a babysitter with the wages I was making, but I had no choice but to stay there."

This is the crux of the labor issues in the fashion industry. Management understands that the need for work is often greater than the number of jobs available and uses this disparity against workers who are asking for the most basic rights. This has been exploited by factories for decades, and it's how they went from working with unions to circumventing them to hire vulnerable workers who could not fight back. And it's more than just low pay that these workers are up against. According to Maria, conditions at the factory were so awful that they often cost her money.

"There's usually no cleaning happening in the factories. Sometimes the kitchen or the area for meals are dirty. Sometimes you even have employers who don't have a dining area, and so they [employees] would have to eat outside in the parking lot. Or try to find a corner for you to sit down and eat. Sometimes you will see rats running underneath your feet or near tables because the factory is so dirty and they're not cleaning enough," she said. "The employers don't buy toilet paper, and there's no soap in the workplaces, so sometimes we have to bring our own soap and toilet paper into work and sometimes they only sweep one time per week, and so the floor is filled with all the fabrics of the garments, and the trash ends up accumulating because a lot of workers take food to work and nobody throws out the trash until that time to clean and that happens once per week."

The sewing machines were broken too. "If your machine breaks down, you just have to wait for the employer to repair the machine, and that usually takes a really long time for them to fix your machine. When you're getting paid per piece, that means I'm not making any money."

In all of those years of protests and music videos and sweatshop raids and empty promises, Maria and her colleagues continued to make $300 a week working twelve-hour days right in Los Angeles. It's illegal, but the brands have no interest in stopping it. "If the inspector is coming, they usually close the factories and they go home to avoid getting any citations because they know that if they get cited, they close their shop and open somewhere else. There are a few days, sometimes weeks, though, where we don't work, and we don't get paid."

This is why worker-led organizing in Los Angeles has become more important than ever before. The Garment Worker Center, a worker rights organization whose mission is to organize low-wage garment workers in Los Angeles, is leading the fight to end what is referred to as the piece rate in Los Angeles. SB-62, which passed in September 2021, makes it illegal for brands in California to pay workers by the garment they make and instead would force them to pay minimum wage.

"You could be undocumented, you could have legal status, you could be a U.S. citizen, if you're working in these industries, you're going to come out with cheap wages and exploitation," Narro explained. He went on to say that we shouldn't be looking for "Made in America" tags because it doesn't mean anything until more bills pass and we have guarantees that workers' rights are prioritized. Instead of seeing that label as propaganda that American is better, we should use it as a basis to push further. We should ask where in the United States that piece of clothing is being made and by whom. Are those workers unionized, or does the factory have certifications to prove that they are adhering to good labor practices? When something is made in the United States, can we make sure that those workers are being treated with respect before we accept a premium price and a marketing campaign around American-made goods?

I believe we can. The reason SB-62 is so different than the legislation in the '90s is that there is a heightened awareness. Workers have spoken out publicly about their low wages, organizers have put together campaigns that directly target Governor Gavin Newsom, and consumers are getting involved.

"The greatest development twenty years later has been the social consciousness of people like yourself," Narro told me, referring to the fact that I work in fashion magazines that typically didn't cover sweatshops or labor issues. He went on, "Now there are 170 groups coming out, forming their coalition to counter the narrative put forth by the brands and by the chamber of commerce." That narrative is unsurprising and based on nothing except fear. The chamber of commerce, for example, claims that the bill will kill jobs, which is simply not true. California as a whole has one of the highest minimum wages in the country and has a steady employment rate of 93 percent. Of course, not all garment work in the United States is in Los Angeles—there are factories in New York City, Texas, Washington State, and more. However, of the 200,000 people employed in U.S. garment factories, 50,000 cutting and sewing operators are concentrated in California. If we want to make "Made in America" something that means sweatshop-free, fixing the practices that had been allowed to continue in Los Angeles for decades is one of the best ways to do it.

The garment factory floor is a metaphor for the way we view labor and profit in the United States. Those at the bottom of the organization chart are perceived as disposable cogs in a

machine that serves the people at the top. This is what radical-
ized workers around the country in 2021: service and manufacturing employees saw their wages stagnate while executives
made more money than ever. Now that more of us see just how
pervasive the problem is, we need to reframe our idea about
what "Made in America" means. "Made in America" means
that the clothing was manufactured in the United States,
though some of the materials and pieces may not have been. It
means that the clothing was made by a person that *should* have
all the same rights that any other worker in the United States
has, but it doesn't mean that they do because of the ways that
companies have exploited contracting laws and immigrants
for decades. It also means it was made by someone whose skill
and worth is no more or less than those of any other person in
the world and that they should all be treated with dignity and
respect.

3

Where Was Fashion's #MeToo?

I WAS STANDING IN MY BATHROOM, HALF-ASLEEP AND BRUSHING my teeth, the first time I saw someone post about #MeToo on Twitter. The tweet caught my attention because it was created by a friend who doesn't really use social media in any way other than to show off pictures of her art. No details, just two short words we all so often blurt out casually. It was followed by hundreds of likes and comments from other people repeating the hashtag almost as though someone had copy-pasted the original post from a bunch of burner accounts. Admittedly, I was confused. I washed my face, now racking my brain for what her post could mean as the hot water splashed in the sink. Eventually I lay down in bed and continued scrolling through my feeds on Twitter and Facebook noticing the hashtag over and over again. Somehow in the few short hours that I had been off my phone a shift had happened, and by the next day, a new "era" had begun forcing society to look directly at how some men had wielded unchecked power for decades without any consequence.

Although Tarana Burke started the #MeToo movement in 2006, the phrase would not be widely popularized until 2017, when Hollywood actress Alyssa Milano tweeted (initially without citation of Burke's decade of work) to call attention to the universality of sexual harassment. In response, thousands of women said "me too" as we remembered the awkward and unwanted shoulder rub from a former boss, a demoralizing pet name like sweetheart from a teacher, or the gross, terrifying feeling that came with a catcall when you were only twelve years old. Many recalled abuse as serious as rape that went untold for fear of retribution or not being believed. Some spoke about how young girls are told to wear longer skirts and looser tops, while the boys who harassed them were simply "doing what boys do." It was as if the earth had opened up and allowed us to see another layer most of us already understood was there, but never talked about.

Male executives at tech brands like Uber, Amazon, and Google faced backlash from women across the companies alleging mistreatment and harassment through heartbreaking open letters and social media posts. In sports, brave gymnasts came forward about the years of sexual abuse they endured from their former team doctor Larry Nassar, who was eventually convicted of rape in 2020 and sentenced to life in prison. Women and nonbinary people in the military reported incidents where they were groped, assaulted, and abused, but never allowed to talk about it for fear of repercussions, or they were silenced through preferential treatment of their male counterparts. It was devastating, sure, but simultaneously, what once seemed like a career-ending move now seemed to be part of a cosmic shift and the start of healing for those who had been silenced.

In Hollywood, famed producer Harvey Weinstein became the face of abusive men when dozens of actresses detailed devastating stories about rape and harassment. His behavior was well known, but was simply swept under the rug with money, fear tactics, and nondisclosure agreements. Still, he was a celebrated man who would sit front row at the Oscars, laughing alongside other famous people, some of them knowing his secrets but afraid of what would happen if they didn't participate in his ruse. He asserted his power over the women he worked with at those ceremonies, pressuring them to wear Marchesa gowns on the red carpet, the brand designed by his then-wife, Georgina Chapman. According to several publicists, Weinstein reportedly threatened actress Sienna Miller, making it clear that he would be upset if she didn't wear the brand to the premiere of the 2007 film *Factory Girl*.[1] Weinstein could make or break careers, and one can imagine that upsetting him over a premiere dress is not a move you want to make. The aftermath for Marchesa was mixed, but indicative of a larger story that was about to unfold around #MeToo and fashion.

At the start, celebrities who once found their names on best-dressed lists wearing Marchesa were quiet about it. There appeared to be a silent understanding that wearing the brand might send an unintended message: a dress that once was the epitome of glamour had now become a symbol of coercion, guilt, and sometimes shame. Soon, though, it became evident that the brand wouldn't be going anywhere. Anna Wintour even wrote an op-ed defending Chapman from those who said she should close her brand for good: "Blaming her for any of it, as too many have in our gladiatorial digital age, is wrong," the famed editor in chief wrote. But is it so far-fetched to think that a movement about autonomy couldn't also apply to a dress?

The world of fashion couldn't keep #MeToo at bay for long— and celebrities certainly understood that fashion could tell a story loudly and clearly. In 2018, when the first Golden Globe Awards following the #MeToo explosion took place, some actresses resolved to raise awareness for Time's Up, a new organization created to support victims of sexual harassment in the workplace.

I have covered red carpets as an editor for the past decade. At magazines like *Teen Vogue* and *InStyle*, where I worked, red carpets are our biggest night to direct traffic to the company's website. It's fashion, glamour, and ridiculousness all wrapped up in a five-hour special that audiences love to read about. My side of the evening is decidedly less spectacular, and usually involves me in my pajamas, hunched over a laptop with the television blaring in the background so I can hear people say which designer made which actress's dress before I hit "publish" on my story. Usually, I'm writing anywhere from ten to fifteen stories a night, describing dresses in detail and trying to come up with silly headlines that include some sort of metaphor the rest of the editors and I will get a kick out of. A personal favorite of mine: calling Lili Reinhart's high-low gown a "mullet dress."

The night of the 2018 Globes, things were different. I was still in my pajamas, hunched over my computer, but we were no longer talking about clothing in the same way. There were no punchy headlines or labels to mention. The celebrities walked the carpet with serious expressions on their faces, ready to be asked about the movement. They all still wore designer dresses—Emilia Clarke wore Miu Miu, Nicole Kidman stunned in a Givenchy gown, and Dakota Johnson looked so incredible in a Gucci dress I could have fallen out of my chair when I saw it—but none of them wanted to talk about their outfits.

There were a few reasons for this. First, it was to show a sign of solidarity against harassment in the workplace and equal pay for women. Second, they were making the point that men get asked about their work and women are asked about their dresses. The two people who didn't participate in the black dress protest that night stood out and made themselves tabloid fodder whether they meant to or not. A scene that would typically have been a sea of color, lace, glitter, and tulle was now devoid of it all. Just black dresses and suits that gave off a tone of seriousness and reverence.

It was a powerful moment for Hollywood and for fashion, but it stopped short of a true reckoning with how deeply the problem of gender-based violence and harassment impacts the entire industry, especially for the most vulnerable. The #MeToo and Time's Up movement didn't make it to the places where those beautiful black gowns and suits were made. I'm not suggesting the actresses shouldn't have been there celebrating their own achievements—in a way, that would have been antithetical to the whole point—nor am I suggesting that they are responsible for abuse in other industries. Fashion could have been an entry point to talk about the marginalized people who were not reached by the movement. But instead, it was a well-intentioned but still performative act that missed a pervasive issue. In an industry where most of the workforce is female, sexual harassment and abuse is rife throughout the factory floor, from the luxury business to fast fashion.

When I first began researching this book, I exchanged texts with a woman in the Dominican Republic who wanted to tell her story of working in the fashion industry. She began working at age eighteen to help her mother support her siblings; her town was once known for being a denim capital, and brands like Levi's subcontracted with several factories in her neighborhood.

When we agreed to speak, I thought she was going to give me

information about the low wages and poor factory conditions, but instead she led with this: "Factory conditions were not very favorable, but it was the only thing we had here in Villa Altagracia. Many times the superiors wanted some women to have sex to get the job. They also prevented studying [for school]." It's not that I didn't expect all sorts of abuse to be taking place in garment factories, but I was learning just how bad it was for women. The gender-based discrimination that goes on in some of these places is not only about the lack of respect we give people turning the gears of fashion elsewhere, it's often a life-threatening aspect of the work. The prevalence of assault and harassment is egregious, and it's a direct result of how obtuse the industry can be about its own problems.

Another example came from a woman named Lorena, who I spoke to on the phone in 2020. She used to work in a factory just ten miles from where all of the celebrities were photographed protesting sexual assault on the Golden Globes carpet in Beverly Hills.

"I love clothes," Lorena told me one evening after a day at work. She uttered these three words inside a raspy laugh. "I am fifty years old, but I don't like to dress like I am. I dress casual." Lorena is a garment worker who grew up in El Salvador and began working at a factory in her hometown when she was twenty-two years old, after her daughter's father died. She had children and a mother to take care of and needed money. Jobs were hard to come by, but, "thank God," she said, with a deep breath as she recalled her life back then, there was one at a factory. In the beginning, her job was to insert the tags that tell you the piece of clothing she was working on was "Made in El

Salvador." Although she worked from four in the morning until five or six at night, Lorena made less than a dollar for every grueling hour—not nearly enough to support her children.

"It was poverty," she explained. Then, Lorena heard that in the United States, you could work in the garment factories and make more than what she was making in El Salvador. So she packed up her bags, left her family behind, and made her way to Los Angeles. When she got there, Lorena's cousin took her to the factory where she worked and helped her get a job. Lorena was a trimmer at first, until she got her own sewing machine. She worked sixty hours and made $125 to $250 a week—about a fifth of the minimum wage in the city. Still, it was more than what she made in the factories in El Salvador, so she stayed and worked.

Lorena was matter-of-fact when she talked about her experience in the United States. She told me about the man who managed the factory where she was most recently employed. His name came out of her mouth sharp and cut like a knife. She said it again to make sure I heard it. "Noé," she repeated, her voice lifting for clarity. "His name was Noé." Noé harassed her daily. He would ask for dates, kisses, and sex in exchange for a break. A break that she needed after hours of difficult, taxing work on a sewing machine. Most days, Lorena never saw daylight.

He told her that if she wanted a "better job," she knew how to get it: by sleeping with him. He would constantly ask her for sex, telling her that it would make her life at the factory easier. Often, she feared for her safety, but still she was able to dodge his inappropriate advances. Other coworkers at the factory were treated in the same way, and many of them weren't able to walk away from Noé. They had to "give in," she said. "To survive."

"Noé," Lorena said again, louder this time.

I realized that she was repeating his name because she wanted to make it clear that he no longer had power over her. Saying his name with conviction to a person she knows will put what he did in writing is her way of reclaiming what he took from the women at the factory. Noé would put his hand on Lorena's ribs or back while she was working. Touching her inappropriately, not caring if she was uncomfortable. As she described this detail, there was an unnerving sobriety in her voice. There was no quiver or hesitation, just a resolve to tell her story. "I would tell him no, I would try to stop the advances, but, even then, whenever he would drop off my work at my station, he would touch me," she said. "I would say, 'You need to respect me!' but it didn't change things."

Lorena spoke firmly about the abuse she endured at the factory throughout our entire conversation, but noted that she never told anyone at work what she was going through. Like the millions of women who kept these stories stashed away for fear of retribution before the #MeToo movement offered them new forms of protection, Lorena knew what would happen if she told on her boss. "Even if it was possible, I would lose my job," Lorena reasoned when I asked her what would have happened if she had told someone. In her position, retaliation is not an unspoken threat; real threats of violence or removal were understood by everyone in garment factories. Losing a job that already pays you poverty wages would be devastating, and the managers won't hesitate to kick you out on the spot.

The brands whose clothes she was making weren't going to help either. "Only Noé checked our work. No one else ever came," she explained. She didn't even know what brands she was working for most of the time if she wasn't able to see the labels. Often brands will claim transparency by listing the city, like Los Angeles, where the clothing is manufactured, but no representative from the company ever steps foot in the factory to see what's going on. According to many of the workers I spoke to, representatives from the brands are led around by management, and they don't speak to the workers. The real story is never heard.

When we spoke in April 2021, Lorena was still unemployed because of the COVID-19 pandemic. She had contracted the virus in early May 2020, and it put her out of work. She hadn't paid her rent in months and subsisted on free food from neighborhood charities. Though she wanted to work again, she was hesitant about returning to a place where she may still be sexually harassed. The time away from her work allowed her the space to reassess some of the ways she had been treated by factory management. "I will not let anybody harass me and I will make sure that I'm treated with respect," she declared. "And if I have to file a complaint for harassment, I will."

She knew, though, that fighting back in garment factories can be incredibly dangerous. Just a week before our conversation, Jeyasre Kathiravel, a twenty-year-old woman in Tamil Nadu, India, was found murdered. Jeyasre was a garment

worker who made clothing at Natchi Apparels, a supplier
for H&M. Her male manager, who her family says had been
harassing her for months, admitted to killing her and leaving
her body on a farm near her parents' house. The manager was
only charged with murder, but Kathiravel's parents say that
she had been raped as well. "My daughter told me that she was
being tortured at work," her mother said following her death.
She also explained that Jeyasre had attempted to report what
was happening to her at work and nothing was done. What's
more is that according to the Tamil Nadu Textile and Common Labour Union, Jeyasre was not the only woman who was
harassed by the managers at the factory.[2]

Silence is a common response for most sexual assault victims, women and men equally, because promises of justice or
restitution are so rare and often go unfulfilled. For garment
workers, silence is even more pervasive, because retaliation
is not as simple as getting fired and then moving on to a new
job. Managers in some factories have been accused of threatening workers with serious physical and verbal abuse. In 2019,
a complaint about a supervisor in a factory that made clothing for Vans and Nautica in Peenya, India, described a situation in which a worker tried to speak out about being sexually
harassed and was chased and beaten by the staff. The report
read: "The General Manager summoned her, abused her verbally and asked her to obey commands and never question
any of the supervisors. He threatened her and took his boots
off to beat her. The garment worker made a run for it and
at the behest of the GM 20 men holding different supervi-
sory roles in the factory chased her down and pulled apart

her clothes and scratched her even as her colleagues came to her rescue."[3]

Following the assault, the police discovered that dozens of women at the factory had tried to report harassment and had been ignored. Many of the workers claimed that their supervisor had taken obscene photos of them, and some claimed he would watch pornography while at work. According to a worker who spoke with the press at the time, the women at the factory did report the harassment through a suggestion box, but found that their anonymous notes had been thrown out or ignored.

Factory garment workers are not treated as employees of the brands they are making clothing for and therefore don't receive the same protection as someone who works at the parent corporation. After Jeyasre's murder, H&M made a statement that they were investigating the matter, but such investigations typically happen only after someone has already been victimized. In 2018, Global Labor Justice published a report featuring interviews with more than five hundred women who were at "daily risk" of sexual harassment in factories in Bangladesh, Cambodia, India, Indonesia, and Sri Lanka that make clothing for H&M. In the aftermath, a spokesperson for H&M said they would review each level of their manufacturing to stop abuse before it happened. "All forms of abuse or harassment are against everything that H&M group stands for," the spokesperson said at the time. Clearly, the company's review did not prevent Jeyasre's murder.

The response read like the typical refrain of corporations following a problematic headline-making incident. We don't tolerate what happened [check!]. We'll look into it ourselves and report back [check, check!]. For the most part it works: the public moves on from the story, and the brand gets to throw money at the problem and put their misdoings in the past. Unfortunately, for the people it matters to most, it always resurfaces. And that's what happened with Jeyasre. Her manager was not a bad apple, this was a systemic issue.

Corporations and their brands, by definition, don't have a moral compass—but people do. It's clear that without sustained backlash, the brands will do what they need to do to make the problem go away without actually getting to the root of the issue. Immediately following Jeyasre's death, H&M released a new collaboration with an incredibly talented Irish designer, Simone Rocha. It was part of a larger series that has seen collections from Moschino, Comme des Garçons, Versace, and other major luxury brands. It's a wildly successful franchise for H&M because it gets tons of media attention for how it has democratized fashion, making an inaccessible brand affordable enough for a middle-class person to purchase.

The Simone Rocha x H&M pieces that came out in 2021 were undeniably pretty and, like clockwork, every single magazine published a story about them. Poufy-sleeved blouses mixed perfectly with tartan pants, and beautiful organza dresses, were like the life-size version of something you'd see on a demented doll packed away in an attic. The line was cool and affordable, the perfect combination for most women's magazine audiences.

When I was at *InStyle*, the fashion commerce team wrote two stories about it, one about the news of the collaboration and another story that included ways to buy it. All of the other magazines—*Elle*, *Vogue*, *Glamour*, and *Harper's Bazaar*—ran similar stories. And why wouldn't they? The clothing looked great, the photos were good, and H&M is accessible. Influencers with millions of followers also promoted the collaboration by posting perfectly edited photos of themselves wearing the outfits, directing followers to purchase them. None of this was abnormal. It's a cycle I have participated in throughout my whole career. What struck me during this particular launch was the timing, and the juxtaposition with Jeyasre's murder. It was as if she had vanished, even as the fashion industry at large poured its energy into a pretty dress—a dress that women just like Jeyasre had stitched together while enduring sexual harassment and starvation wages. It reminded me that celebrities could take a stand by wearing all black on a red carpet—and we could all remain ignorant of the bigger picture, the real #MeToo story in fashion.

It's easier to see something palatable than to recognize our own complicity in the system.

Though it may not have been intentionally timed, H&M could count on the fact that the publicity around the new collaboration would likely reach the masses, while only a few people would speak about the news of Jeyasre's death. The company made a settlement with her family, once again promised to do better, and the media moved on from the rape and murder of a woman who made the clothing they are still selling us.

Erasing Lorena's humanity is something that these brands do purposefully. Her skill, her sweat, and sometimes her trauma is stitched into every garment that ends up hanging on a rack for $9.99. Workers are far removed from the brands they are making clothing for, a fact that allows blame or responsibility for their treatment to be pushed off onto someone else. The brands prefer it this way, because fixing these issues would implicate a larger cultural problem throughout the industry. When certain photographers and executives were forced to step down from their powerful positions, we could point the finger at their behavior. They were the "bad apples" of fashion. But when you look at entire suppliers engaging in harassment and gender-based violence, then the problem is systemic. We need to overhaul the relationship between the garment workers and the labels they are sewing. That's where all of us, fashion lovers, buyers, influencers, and journalists can come in: we can push brands to fix their relationship with factories and make the necessary changes to keep workers safe.

In May 2021, leggings brand Fabletics, founded by Kate Hudson, decided to cut ties with a factory in Africa after a *Time* report discovered rampant harassment of workers by supervisors.[4] In the investigation, thirteen women said that "their underwear and vulvas are often exposed during routine daily searches by supervisors," and three alleged that they had been sexually harassed in other ways. Fabletics responded by suspending orders and conducting an investigation into the matter before they eventually stopped working with that specific factory. They also claimed they would try to join the Lesotho agreement, which was created two years prior in response to harassment found at factories making clothing for Levi's and other major U.S.-based companies.

Fabletics' response was the right one—and the company moved quickly. Within mere hours of the report the brand was "taking a stand." The female empowerment–focused brand and Kate Hudson herself certainly don't want to be associated with gender-based violence. Customers can use that to their advantage: pushing a brand to change its system in a public way is something they may well respond to.

But the Fabletics story also indicates a deeper problem. The company claimed to have a rigorous auditing process *before* the harassment allegations took place—and yet this still happened. As I write this almost a year after the *Time* report, Fabletics only has their "commitments" listed on their website. There are no suppliers available for customers to look into and no worker testimonials. Just promises. We can push them on this publicly through posting on social media and asking them why they haven't been transparent about their process. We can also look to organizations like the Model Alliance, which works to end sexual harassment in the modeling industry, and Remake, a nonprofit that educates people about gender and climate justice in fashion. We have to fight fire with fire. If Fabletics wants to be the brand that helps women be their best selves and markets their leggings as such, we should hold them to it publicly. And we should do the same for every brand we patronize as consumers.

Public pressure can work. In Jeyasre's case, H&M eventually agreed to implement gender-based violence training and an anonymous reporting structure for workers. None of that would have happened if consumers didn't show their support for and awareness of the changes workers were asking for.

4

The Illusion of Choice

It was a busy Tuesday in 2018 when my friend Madison texted me. "Call me; I have news," she wrote. When I finally got a chance, I found a small conference room in the Condé Nast One World Trade Center offices and dialed her number. "Oh my god," she said the second she picked up. "I'm going to be in a PrettyLittleThing campaign." Her voice was filled with excitement as she detailed how she was going to fly to Los Angeles within the week, along with a group of models for the brand's International Women's Day campaign.

Just a few months before that, Madison had written a story that I assigned to her for *Teen Vogue* about the lack of disability representation in fashion. "Most clothing is made for people who stand, and for people who sit all day—like I do—things get awkward. High-waisted pants bunch in the front and short dresses are a wardrobe malfunction waiting to happen," she wrote in the piece. She went on, "Somewhere along the way, people like me were taken out of the equation of clothing design." A person in the marketing department at PrettyLittleThing had read the story and wanted her to be involved in their newest campaign, promoting a diverse group of women. For Madison, the opportunity to model was a chance to be a part of a change for herself and for her community—especially with a brand that had very quickly become one of the most popular fast fashion companies globally.

PrettyLittleThing was created by billionaire heirs Umar and Adam Kamani, sons of Mahmud Kamani, who founded the Boohoo Group in 2006 and acquired a majority stake in PLT in 2016, just four years after its launch. Umar and Adam are the definitions of socialite kids. One scroll through their social media pages, and you'll find photos of them on obscure red carpets wearing expensive suits, kneeling down with friends on the golf course, and, of course, posing in front of cars with their arms crossed. Their brand quickly shot into popularity when their celebrity friends, like Paris Hilton, Sofia Richie (daughter of Lionel Richie), and Kylie Jenner began promoting the collections on social media. They used a formula similar to that of their father's brand: quick, trendy clothing at a very low price. The difference, however, was in the advertising. Alongside flashy images of famous women and heavily Photoshopped influencers wearing sparkly cocktail dresses, there was a social justice marketing initiative soon to be fronted by activists like Madison.

"I wanted to do the campaign because when I was young, I wasn't able to look at a magazine and see somebody that looked like me. I wanted to feel that representation, but it was never there," Madison told me a few years later. When she arrived at the photo shoot, however, it was immediately apparent that they hadn't actually thought about her needs as a disabled woman; they just wanted her image to diversify the reach. "The shoot hashtag was #everybodyinPLT but when we got on set, they immediately were like 'Okay, everybody, you put on this outfit. You put on this outfit.' Except for me, they didn't have anything for me to wear. I showed up to set with little black booties and leggings and a sports tank top, and they didn't ever change me out of my leggings and boots. It made no sense," she explained.

During the shoot, Madison decided not to speak up about what she was experiencing—she had the unfair burden of representing her community in something visible and potentially empowering. "There's this weird double-edged sword where I need to be advocating for myself because they need to know how to treat models like me, but on the other hand, if they think that what I need is above and beyond, then they're never going to hire another model in a wheelchair," she said. I could hear the distress in her voice as she recalled this moment. She used the phrase "prima donna" when describing how she felt asking for her most basic human needs, like a wheelchair-accessible taxi.

At one point, it was clear to the makeup artist working with Madison that something wasn't right. The artist told her that she had a relative who also used a wheelchair and through that experience she saw that the brand had not made any accommodations for the model they'd hired. It's not that Madison didn't want to assert herself—she did. It's just that speaking up was risking not just her job, but future jobs for other disabled people, too. The makeup artist told a producer what was going on.

Still, Madison wore her own shoes and pants to go with the "Girl Gang" shirt the brand provided. "It just felt kind of like a lie to say #everybodyinPLT when my body obviously wasn't on their radar. Sure, their clothing is a little baggy, but everything is a little baggy on me. That's just how stuff fits. It sucked because I felt like they must have thought their clothes would just look bad on me. I've never thought that before of myself—I've literally shopped there," she said, her voice now sterner than before. The whole day she had to pose in photos with models who had been dressed by the brand, knowing she would stick out in the pictures. As the only person in a wheelchair, she was front and center, the focal point in this soon-to-be-lauded, inclusive campaign.

A few weeks after returning home from L.A., the photos were released, and they instantly went viral. I was still working at *Teen Vogue* at the time, and this sort of representative advertising was something I would usually cover—sometimes with less scrutiny than I probably should have exercised. I was just so excited to showcase this massive accomplishment for Madison, and I knew that despite what had happened—she told me briefly about it when she got home—she was proud of the photos. I remember looking through the comments on social media and seeing so many people praising the brand for "finally" showing and catering to people in wheelchairs, precisely the reason why she was chosen to be in the photos. Most people didn't realize she wasn't even wearing a PrettyLittleThing outfit.

In the years following, Madison's experience stayed in the back of my mind: we talked about it a few times as friends commiserating about stupid fashion industry bullshit. But in 2020, as the pandemic exposed issues in the fast fashion supply chain, the performative activism of brands felt like a metaphor for something more significant. Because the pandemic was at one of its first peaks in the United States, it was a unique time for activism on social media. After the police murders of George Floyd and Breonna Taylor, hundreds of thousands of people protested in the streets, and others began a movement online. For brands, sidestepping activism was no longer a choice: customers wanted to know where they stood. Many made promises and donations to organizations like Black Lives

Matter, and others attempted to hold themselves accountable by setting diversity goals. These were important and necessary changes, but, glaringly, none of the brands spoke about how the principles of the movements for racial justice applied to the worst parts of their business.

That day on set with Madison was representative of a similar accessibility conundrum in fashion. Having women with diverse bodies in advertisements is simply good business for the brands—there is often no real activism involved, especially when you consider how people in the supply chain are being abused to put out the product. For many customers, shopping fast fashion is not a moral choice between good and bad brands but rather a choice based on which one can best meet your needs. Of course, it was important for Madison to be in that ad and to have other people who use wheelchairs see themselves in her image, but that's just the surface. Behind that smiling photo was a clear example of how brands have exploited our desire to see certain parts of ourselves where historically we haven't been seen. I have burn scars on 20 percent of my body that I used to cover up with long sleeves and pants. Now I see campaigns from fast fashion brands that show off women with similar scars and I wish they'd existed when I was younger, because that would have normalized having scars and other skin blemishes. The other side of this acknowledgment, though, is that I likely would have bought into these brands because of that representation—when there were likely women making the clothing with similar scars caused by the sweatshop where they worked.

International Women's Day, which the PrettyLittleThing

inclusivity campaign was celebrating, started as a labor movement for garment workers. In 1908, 15,000 women marched
in New York City demanding shorter hours and better pay
following the Triangle Shirtwaist Factory fire, which left 146
workers dead. While the cause of the fire is still debated—some
argued it was a fire in the sewing machine engines, others suggested it could have been a lit cigarette thrown in the fabric,
and many felt it could even have been arson—the reason the
fatalities were so high was that the doors were locked to prevent workers from taking breaks. It was a common practice
at the time, despite the long, arduous hours the women were
working inside the factory. In the aftermath of the disaster, the
survivors and other sweatshop workers took to the streets to
demand regulation and better conditions for themselves. They
also started the International Ladies Garment Workers Union
(ILGWU), which became one of the largest labor unions in the
United States.

The irony is that in June 2020, the *Times on Sunday* reported
that workers—mostly women—making clothing for Pretty-
LittleThing in the Boohoo factory in Leicester, were being paid
£3.50, or $4.40, per hour; the national living wage in England
is £8.72, or $10, per hour. They also reported that they were not
being given masks and were not socially distanced within the
factories, allowing for the potential spread of the virus. The
workers were getting sick. In a later follow-up in the *Daily Mail*,
the owner of the factory admitted to the low wages, claiming
that if he didn't keep his costs low, the brand would use someone who could, in a different country. Of course, that problem isn't just bad for the factory; it's the workers who have to

deal with the consequences of this type of competition. "We are treated like donkeys because there are a lot of orders to fill. People are buying more online," one woman who worked at the factory told the paper. "Which means we have to make more clothes. We are put under a lot of pressure to come to work, even if we are not feeling well. The bosses even threaten us with the sack."

Backlash on social media was swift, with many people pointing to the fact that this brand claims inclusivity but doesn't extend those ideals to their workers. As a result, a few months after the report came out, Boohoo claimed to have cut ties with the factory that had been investigated by *The Times*. The company then released a new list of manufacturers they worked with to replace the ones violating labor laws. Unfortunately, it quickly became clear that the new factories were just as problematic. This time, managers were making it seem like they were paying workers the minimum wage by paying them in full and then forcing the workers to pay back the difference on a lower wage. "'They said, you know, 'I can't give you minimum wage, I can't afford to pay you minimum wage because prices are very low in our product,'" a whistleblower told Sky News in July 2021.[1]

A brand that has been using the underpaid labor of women gained accolades and attention for a campaign celebrating the liberation of women—on a holiday begun by sweatshop workers. To do it, they used the image of an underrepresented woman they didn't make an effort to dress in the clothing they were selling. They were using representation and access as a strategy to redirect our focus from the same exploitation women were fighting against over a hundred years ago and to make us feel good about buying into the brand that, by all other standards, is doing the opposite of helping women. We should be educating each other on exactly how these brands are capitalizing on our fight for equal representation. Brands realize they can profit off our desires by offering inexpensive options and inclusive messaging without putting those values into practice with their own workers.

If we want to solve these problems, it's crucial to recognize that standing up against the overconsumption perpetuated by brands like PrettyLittleThing with your dollar is just not the same for everyone. "Buying better" is often touted as an option, but it's only an option for people with money and access. Why should the burden of fixing an entire industry fall on people who don't have the means to invest in a better system through no fault of their own? Not everyone has the luxury of removing themselves from the buying cycle for the greater good. As Madison explained, "A lot of people in my community are living on social security, two in three disabled people live below the poverty line their whole life, and it's because we have to in order to maintain the insurance that funds the machines and medical treatments that keep us alive. So, to afford clothing that is not only ethical but made for our bodies, that is kind of a privilege that not everybody can afford."

The biggest problems concerning access in fashion are options. Fast fashion brands will exploit the fact that the rest of the industry ignores anyone who is not a straight-size person whether or not they have the clothing to cater to their needs.

Essentially, erasure from the industry has given fast fashion a marketing opportunity.

Take, for example, how fast fashion has been able to capitalize on the unwillingness of ethical or small brands to readjust to include more size options. Many brands, like Reformation, offer transparent manufacturing and use buzz words like "sustainability," yet barely make an extra-large size piece of clothing. In the luxury market, you'd be hard-pressed to find one option for anyone over a size 8. Despite one or two exceptions to the arbitrary straight-size rule, the move toward inclusion has been glacial at best, and there is always an excuse. When I have pressed ethical designers about this in the past, the answer is usually that it costs more to make the samples in different sizes. It's this argument that Christian Siriano, one of the only luxury designers to include plus sizes in his collections, addressed head-on in an interview. He explained that it's about effort. "It's definitely harder; it's not the easiest job. And that's really because the process is longer. It's like, you have to fit your clothes on multiple sizes before you actually produce them, which a lot of brands just don't want to do because they don't want to take the time or the money and the resources."

La'Shaunae Steward is a model and influencer who has been working in fashion since 2017 and has been outspoken about the issues with accessibility in the fashion industry. I got to know them when they collaborated with shoe brand Jeffrey Campbell to create a plus-size thigh-high boot. At the time, boots that were essentially pants had become the top trend, worn by everyone everywhere, in no small part due to a high-

ponytailed pop star named Ariana Grande. As a fashion editor, I wrote endlessly about who was wearing them and how to
style them, but there was an expected hole in the market when
it came to where to buy them. Most of these boots were made
by the shoe size, not by the leg size, and the boots for anyone
with thicker thighs were impossible to find.

Before Jeffrey Campbell launched the extended sizes,
La'Shaunae had been given a pair of boots from the brand to
post on their social media. When they took the photos, they
found that the boot's shaft was too small for their ankle and
wouldn't stay up. They had to leave them unzipped in the photos. "It was an outfit of me in a yellow plaid skirt and the boots,
and they never stayed up the entire time. I had this struggle to
keep them up just for the photos, so I wrote about it in the caption," they recalled. Someone at the brand responded by hiring
them to help with a collection of five plus-size shoe styles. It
was a game changer for their career and the first time people
working in fashion, including journalists and stylists, began
paying attention. (Singer Lizzo even wore them.) In the months
that followed the launch, La'Shaunae's following grew from a
few thousand people to over a hundred thousand. They were
in a national campaign for Universal Standard, won *Dazed*
magazine's top 100 influencers contest, and they were all
over the internet as a rising star. Despite these achievements,
they weren't being treated like a successful model by the luxury fashion industry. There were no invites to walk down a
runway, no panels, no editorials, just news stories about how
groundbreaking they were.

"I'm always conflicted when I'm working with fast fashion

brands. The brands underpay the workers. They underpay the creatives that are actually doing the content for them, making a ton of money in the process. But they are the only ones really hiring me," La'Shaunae said. On top of that, they are some of the only brands actually making clothing for them to model. "My entire career has been hard, financially. I just don't have the same opportunities as thin models, so what do you do when these are the only brands reaching out to pay you?" they asked me in that same conversation.

The question doesn't have a straight answer, because the experience La'Shaunae has had with these brands is complicated. Even though the fast fashion brands have given them the opportunities that other ethical and sustainable brands have not, they have also undercut them, paid them less than thin, white influencers, and asked them to do free work for exposure.

Like a lot of other influencers, though, La'Shaunae's following grew when the pandemic began, and as a result they felt they should be paid more. It makes sense, of course: the more eyes on the product, the higher value to the brand, and the compensation should reflect that. At first, they told me, the brand did pay a little bit more for the already agreed-to images. But when those photos went up, the brand explained that they would no longer be paying for the content and instead would just send free products, leaving it up to La'Shaunae to decide if the relationship would continue. "[The brand] said that they would still send me clothes to post without paying me," La'Shaunae said, stressing that the brand cut them off from paid work despite knowing how vulnerable they were in the pandemic. With everything that has happened in the years following that initial pandemic outbreak, it's easy to forget just how vulnerable some people really were. Not only were Black people dying at rates up to three times higher than any other group, there were also disproportionate economic disparities. In July 2020, the Black unemployment rate was 16.7 percent, compared with a white unemployment rate of 14.2 percent.

La'Shaunae's situation is similar to Madison's experience on set: it's not as simple as calling out a brand for taking advantage of them. The fashion industry has a history of ignoring marginalized voices, and when they upset the status quo they run the risk of being silenced. "I usually feel like I'm defending myself when I bring up the issues I face because a lot of people in the industry can't relate to someone who's talking about being left out or excluded for being a size 26 or a size 24 and Black in the fashion industry," La'Shaunae explained. "I have to take what I can get."

Fast fashion brands want to use La'Shaunae's image and following to sell clothing, but they don't actually want to do the work to create lasting relationships or change for the women and nonbinary people they employ. They consistently tokenize the models they work with and get attention for being more diverse. The brands stand on platitudes about inclusion, but they do it in bad faith.

La'Shaunae had been an activist for years and was often ostracized for speaking up. They felt that it wasn't until there was money to be made, or clout to be had, that people in fashion and brands even began to listen. While it may seem ridiculous, it works. Representation for people sizes 16 and above is so hard to come by that even the slightest bit of inclusion gets attention, accolades, and, in turn, customers. It's hard to see the high cost of representation when it's not reflected on the price tag. Fashion Nova, the brand giving La'Shaunae most of their work before the pandemic, is one of the least transparent companies in fashion. Many of the women I spoke with who were being underpaid and mistreated worked in factories in Los Angeles that made Fashion Nova garments. Santa Puac, a garment worker and activist, said there was a time when she was working at a factory that made clothing for the brand seven days a week, offering no extra pay, and that that's why the brand was able to offer accessible options so quickly and cheaply. You can't see that through an influencer's Instagram post, however.

It's important to point out that fast fashion's success is not because marginalized or low-income people are the only people buying in. It's because the corporations take advantage of and perpetuate consumption. They are the ones purposefully using extremely clever marketing to keep us hooked, playing into our best instincts to seek inclusivity and our worst to ignore the larger picture. And for fashion influencers like Madison and La'Shaunae, one of the most challenging parts of working in the industry is that they often find themselves in situations in which there is no winner. They are shamed by activists for working with brands that are harmful to their workers, but if they don't work with these brands in some way, they don't work. La'Shaunae told me that just because they get some work from recognizable brands doesn't mean that they aren't still struggling. Furthermore, they feel the ire of people who tell them to stop working with the brands. The choice is not the same for every model.

"I see this shame-driven argument all the time on social media, especially from straight-size models and fashion influencers, basically shitting on the fat influencers and fat models that wear ASOS, PrettyLittleThing, Missguided, other fast fashion brands," they explained. "But these girls don't understand that it's most plus-size models' only option. We're bigger than them, so even if we wanted to get designer jobs, they quite literally don't make clothing for us. It's not the best, but it's all we have unless we thrift, which is also very hard." Often thrift or consignment is postured as a better way to shop and an alternative to fast fashion, but just like the rest of the industry, there are people left out of the conversation. When you consider that catering to sizes above an 8 is still a contemporary concept, there really isn't much for plus-size shoppers in the way of vintage. What's more is that the pieces that were being made were often ill-fitting or not trendy. When I look at the dozens of Instagram secondhand shops I follow, almost none of them carry large sizes. How are people supposed to feel like they have that option when, optically, it's pretty clear that the world of secondhand shopping was made for small people?

It's not enough to just put women in advertisements and call it a job well done. Madison explained it perfectly to me toward the end of our conversation. "Inclusion is more than just having a seat at the table. It's being listened to, it's being incorporated in all aspects of what the brand is standing for. It's not using disabled and marginalized people as props to sell clothing."

For customers, it's about having a little bit more nuance in the way we advocate to slow down the consumption of fast fashion. You don't know why someone is shopping at Fashion Nova, and shaming someone for making that choice can be ableist. Exploiting the vulnerabilities of size and access has been a tool for growth at the expense of the very people brands pretend to care about, and pointing the finger at each other allows them to refocus blame away from themselves. Instead, we have to look at the industry as a whole and understand why we have allowed brands that have built their wealth on the abuse of women throughout the supply chain to be the arbiters of inclusivity.

From the media side, I can tell you, there is so much work to be done. While you may have seen incremental changes—a plus-size model on the cover of a magazine and other "firsts" here and there—it's not what it seems.

In 2018, I was at a pitch meeting for a September cover. There were several senior members of the team in the room, and we were all trying to pick who we would feature in a package about bodies. Some famous activists' names got thrown around, and it seemed like everyone was on the same page about the message we wanted to send. That is, until someone mentioned having a plus-size model on the cover. The woman sitting across from me, who had a lot of power, sat up in her chair, interrupting the conversation we were having because she felt she couldn't let us go on without mentioning that she didn't want to promote "that."

"What is 'that'?" I remember someone asking. She just shrugged because she knew she couldn't say it even though her tone spoke volumes.

A few of us looked at each other, disgusted and puzzled. We were supposed to be the magazine that was radicalizing what fashion should look like. We were telling young people to say "fuck you" to unrealistic and misogynist standards, but, behind-the-scenes, we were perpetuating them. A few people tried to change the subject quickly, pretending like the plus-sized person was an option that would be considered, but still the stench of what had just been said hung in the air. I learned within the week that the person I wanted never got their cover, and instead three palatably diverse models who had big contracts were hired and we were never asked our thoughts about it again. It was so incredibly disheartening, because while I thought that real work was being done to change who we see legitimized in the fashion industry, we were nowhere near achieving our goals of inclusivity.

Attitudes like the one displayed by the powerful woman in that meeting are pervasive, and they seep into every single aspect of the industry, all the way down to department stores, most of which are not even structured to accommodate people with mobility differences. My mother and I used to love going shopping together. In the last couple of years, however, her disability has gotten worse and she needs a wheelchair to get around. We went to Macy's one afternoon, and as we got toward the entrance I realized it was going to be impossible to get her through the double door without anyone helping me. Once we got inside, I would have to park her chair in the aisle while I went and pulled things out to bring over to show her. Even more than that, if she had been by herself most of the racks would have been too tall to reach and she wouldn't have been able to pull anything down. So yes, shopping online is easier for her.

The bottom line is that it's okay to get excited about representation, but there is no reason to clap. Simply including more people in their advertising is not something these brands should be rewarded for, especially when they use it to overshadow the issues that are perpetuated in the workforce. They should be representing people; they should be offering diverse sizing and accessibility options.

"I feel like in a lot of ways brands jump at this idea that they can look really inclusive and look really woke in a way that tries to say, 'How can we be, you know, guilty of these horrible things if we're doing this amazing great thing?' But it's like we need to stop looking at inclusion as going above and beyond and start looking at inclusion as what is just expected," Madison said succinctly. "If you're not inclusive, you should be looked down on, but if you are inclusive, you should not be praised for doing what you should have done from the start."

5

Influenced

INFLUENCE IN FASHION IS AN ELUSIVE CONCEPT. SURE, THERE are quantifiable metrics on impressions, link clicks, and views, but it's difficult to describe the "it" factor that makes someone so intrigued by how a stranger dresses.

For me, "it" was always present in child star turned fashion designer Mary Kate Olsen. Olsen was an integral part of the paparazzi-obsessed culture of the early 2000s, and her photo was everywhere. Her thin frame was the topic of invasive and problematic tabloid fodder splashed across magazines at the checkout aisle in the grocery store, and her messy style had become a cultural phenomenon. The early social media site Tumblr had dozens of blogs dedicated to breaking down every outfit she wore, and there were forums for fans to talk about them together. Whenever a small glimpse of her showed up in a magazine, I would cut it out and glue it into a collage that I hung on my wall. The boy band posters of my preteen years had been replaced by pictures of someone representing my new love: fashion.

I loved the way a baggy flannel shirt became a dress with fishnets or how wobbly legs appeared in platform boots as Mary Kate walked to a downtown New York restaurant or out of a club filled with supermodels. To me, she was otherworldly. Her bicep bangles and silicon bracelets seeped into my impressionable heart and led me to the type of fashion I would grow to love. One day, she stepped out wearing a cherry-colored leather jacket over a green American Apparel hoodie. Underneath, she wore a white shift dress and brown cowboy boots. The outfit had a tinge of absurdity, yet she looked so chic as she stared into the paparazzi lenses with an uncomfortable smile.

After seeing the picture, I could not stop thinking about that jacket.

The thing about being a human, with our basic need to feel accepted, is that we can be so captivated by someone who represents what we want to be that we literally buy in. Especially during vulnerable periods of growth in our teens and early twenties, this desire drives us—and fashion brands will use it to their advantage. For me, it was that cherry jacket that represented everything I wanted to be: fashionable, respected, and not sitting in a cold classroom in upstate New York. So I looked everywhere for it. I had a friend drive me to the Salvation Army (because I was *that* friend who didn't have a car or drive), where we found a ton of different old man coats lined up on a rack in the back. I combed through them, noting a rip in one, a button missing from another. None of them captured the look I wanted. The jacket I wanted had to be trendy and fitted, and vintage would not do.

Eventually, after school one day, I went to a bizarre store called Steve and Barry's. It was upstairs in the back corner of a mostly empty 1.3 million-square-foot mall about a half hour from where I lived. The mall was on a main road filled with suburban restaurant staples like Chili's and Buca di Beppo, and the store itself was across from the back entrance of a Christmas Tree Shop where carts spilled over into the empty mall hallway. It had huge a wide-open door that featured the brand's blue wavy block letter logo across the entire transom like it was some sort of promised land of cheap clothing. And similar to other fast fashion stores of its time, the store was constantly a mess of fabric that had been picked over and thrown around by other customers. Naturally, everything was always marked down.

You could find unofficial merchandise for sports teams for under $5 and racks of jewelry that offered combination sales of five pieces for $15. More important, there were also random contemporary collections fronted by celebrities like Sarah Jessica Parker and Venus Williams. When I went in that day, I saw a rack of clothing designed by actress Amanda Bynes. Bynes was at the height of her career coming off of several hit rom-coms like *What a Girl Wants* and *She's the Man*. She was funny, famous, and attractive, making her the perfect candidate to design a fashion collection aimed at teenagers. The line she created was called "Dear," and it was complete with all the styles she and every other young starlet in 2006 wore. Deep V-neck sweaters, empire-waist tunics, graphic thermals, and hooded cardigans lined the walls from front to back as Amanda's smiling face gazed down at me from an advertisement. On one of the racks, a fitted brown faux-leather jacket was marked down to $16.98. The coat had silver hardware that was so light and cheap you could tell it would patina if the slightest moisture was in the air. Still, to me it was perfect. The next day, I wore the jacket to a friend's house, over the hoodie, just like Mary Kate, and I felt as cool as a sixteen-year-old could feel. I remember sitting in my friend's backyard staring straight at the table, then looking around to see if my friends saw me as I saw myself at that moment. Maybe they could see me as someone different—someone who didn't need their approval because I already had it from Mary Kate.

In the grand scheme of influencer culture, my story is

inconsequential. You probably have a similar one with an outfit worn by someone else. A very famous person I liked wore
a jacket, so I bought a version of it that I could afford because
another famous person had verified its coolness. There are so
many factors that go into the reason I decided to spend my
money on various pieces of clothing or accessories, and not the
least of them is seeing someone else wear it first. Even now,
I have an entire folder on Instagram where I save pictures of
outfits that I like; it's mostly pictures of Zoë Kravitz. Influence
is not that complicated, and it's been a strategy used by brands
for a century, but in the last four decades, it's been perfected.

This interaction with fashion and celebrity is what fashion
marketing is built on. Take Kylie Jenner, for example. Arguably she's one of the most influential people in the world, and
a lot of that has been determined by her ability to sell clothing
and makeup. Before the success of her makeup line Kylie Cos-
metics, she tested this power with fast fashion. In 2016, at just
nineteen years old, she made a post on Instagram that made an
almost comically big splash. "Obsessed with my new @fashion-
nova jeans," she wrote in the caption, punctuating the sentence
with an unsubtle peach emoji. In the image, posted initially
to her Instagram, but still plastered all over Fashion Nova's
website years later, Jenner sits with her body turned toward
a window, as she looks back over her shoulder at the camera.
Her hair is long and silky as it cascades over her shoulders. The
jeans in question make her seem impossibly curvy, her waist
small, and her hips wide, round, and out of proportion like a
Barbie. While most of her fans won't shell out for Fendi bags,
have a mansion with perfect lighting, or a gym or chef, what

they can have are those $29 jeans. They can taste the fabulous, beautiful life for the same price as a takeout dinner.

I remember this post so well because I was writing fashion at *Teen Vogue* when it happened. It was a big deal—like, drop everything and get this story up on the website big deal— because anything she wore, especially if there was an ounce of controversy around it, was a guaranteed hit story with hundreds of thousands of clicks. The interesting thing about it was that it was an advertisement—it wasn't like she just had on a cute outfit. She was paid to wear those jeans and yet the mere fact that she was wearing them was newsworthy. Everything else was overlooked in favor of the influence her name had in fashion.

What Kylie didn't mention in her ad was why those jeans were so cheap, or how those jeans were kept in stock despite thousands of sales. No one expects her to, either, because validating a purchase of cheap clothing is her job and she's doing exactly what she was hired to do. With only five words, a coy smile, and 2.6 million likes, Kylie became an integral part of the influencer-led fast fashion marketing strategy.

Even now, with everything we've learned about social media in the years since my Steve and Barry's purchase or that Kylie Jenner advertisement, not much has changed in the way influence is used to sell clothing. If you think about your social media habits, the strategy is already part of your life. Subconsciously and reflexively, you pick up your phone. You're in the middle of watching something on television, and you're getting bored. You're waiting for the water to boil so you can make some pasta and use your phone to fill the space. You're trying to fall asleep, but you only need one more moment of connection. Whatever it is, your thumb goes to an app, and your brain is struck by an array of colors and textures. A pretty, maybe famous, probably rich person is wearing an outfit. It feels good to look at the photo. She looks agreeable and content. The pants fit her nicely, and the caption confirms she is living her best life, and those pants are part of it. So, you click a little more to know where they are from.

To your surprise, they aren't as expensive as they seem, so you think about it. You probably don't buy them at that moment, but those pants are in your head now. The next time you walk to the mirror and look at the pants you pulled from your closet, you think about the pants you saw on your screen. You search them again, and this time you add them to your cart. You get distracted by another notification, and you move on. The next time you're on the app, you encounter another picture. The brightness on the photo is turned up in all the right spots. The coffee in the model's hands looks amazing, and . . . wait a minute . . . there are those pants again. They look good, and what do they cost? Maybe a couple of hours' worth of work? Definitely less than a nice meal. You deserve it. So you buy the pants. I've done this, and you've done this, it's the way it all works now.

We get familiar with people who have influence. We don't know them, but they become a part of our daily lives and, in a lot of ways, part of our friendship circles. We trust their tastes and want to copy the things they wear, but most of us can't afford Balenciaga or Louis Vuitton, so we opt for the more affordable option, hand-picked by them. We use the approval of celebrities to excuse any doubt we might have. All we know is that those jeans look stunning on Kylie, she actually wears them, and they are affordable. What we don't know is what happens in the L.A. factory that makes them.

"Everything is dirty. The bathrooms don't have toilet paper, they don't have soap, they are disgusting," Santa Puac, the Garment Worker Center advocate I met one afternoon in downtown Los Angeles told me. She was referring to the Fashion Nova facility where she formerly worked. "Many times, we are fired from work without getting paid. Sometimes the boss will only give you only half of your pay and force you to work extra for the other half." She also told me that the workers are often verbally abused and berated for things they didn't do. "Sometimes our children get sick and we get fired for going to pick them up. If something is missing in the factory, they will just blame us and take away our pay and fire us," she explained. Santa told me about the expectations put on workers to make as many clothes as possible and when they don't, often for reasons like picking up a sick child from school or taking care of a loved one, they are fired.

There are so many different parts of the story of a fashion brand or trend, and yet there seems to be one narrative that stands out. If influencers and celebrities are metaphorically screaming, then Santa and her colleagues are barely able to whisper. Their story stays quiet and hidden, heard only by the people who will put their ears down to listen; meanwhile, the filtered photos and the perfectly fitted outfits we see on social media dominate the discussion. That's not an accident.

Influencers can shape the way we see a brand in spite of all of the problems they create.

The authority over trends from celebrities and "content creators"—the term an agent for famous TikTokers once asked me to use instead of "influencers"—is demonstrated so clearly in these collaborations and campaigns that we have to wonder why they aren't using their position to call out the practices that allow them to front an ad for $25 jeans.

While we can't solely point the finger at a famous person and charge them with the crimes of a corporation, we can question their motives and urge them to speak against the labor violations these brands commit in order to make enough money to hire them in the first place. Just like what happened when I wrote the story about Kylie's jeans for *Teen Vogue*, celebrity partnerships with fast fashion allow for a simple and effective media strategy that garners a ton of approval for the biggest media brand. These stories legitimize the brand and the collaborations as something that should be respected. And then purchased.

I have participated in this system dozens of times, to the point that I can't even remember all the collaborations I had to cover early in my career. It was usually not even about the brand; it would be an interview with a celebrity in which the connection to fast fashion was slyly slipped in. The access is important for clicks, sure, but it also validates a campaign promoting clothing made by workers who aren't given the same attention or priority as the flashy celebrity whose face is associated with it. Imagine seeing something that caused you harm celebrated by people who also refuse to give your story the respect and time it deserves because celebrity is more valuable. How discouraging would that be?

Perhaps the best and one of the earliest examples of how these competing narratives are sold to the public is the Nike Air Jordan. In 1985, Nike released the Air Jordan 1, created with and advertised by basketball superstar Michael Jordan. At the time, the NBA's official shoe was Converse. Players would step onto the court wearing lace-up All Stars, paired with tall socks accentuated by the super-short shorts they all wore. It was quintessential '70s attire, but the league was due for a shake-up. The '80s were about opulence and color, and the players wanted to show that in their uniforms. It was perfect timing for Nike too, because in order to compete with Reebok and Adidas in the athletic space, they needed to do something splashy. So they offered Jordan a $2.5 million contract he couldn't refuse. The story goes that the basketball player wanted to work with Adidas, his favorite sneaker brand, but his mother told him that turning down Nike would be a huge mistake. She was, of course, completely right; the deal catapulted Michael Jordan and the brand into a level of success that neither had seen before.

When Jordan stepped out onto the court in 1985 wearing the Air Jordan 1s for the first time it changed the fashion world forever. In that moment he became the greatest singular influence on footwear in the world.

Despite rules that said all players had to wear the same shoes, Jordan wore his own anyway, and, as a result, he was fined $5,000 per game, which Nike paid and turned into a marketing opportunity. A 1986 commercial showed Jordan looking straight ahead as he tosses a basketball back and forth in his hands. The camera pans down slowly until it reaches his feet. He's wearing the Air Jordan 1s. "On September 15th, Nike created a revolutionary new basketball shoe," a narrator says over the video. "On September 18th, the NBA threw them out of the game," he continues as two black bars slam over each shoe. "Fortunately, the NBA can't keep you from wearing them," the narrator concludes. The sales goal was $3 million over three years. Nike made $126 million in one year, and, along with Jordan's unprecedented popularity, the sales totals only grew from there.

Sometimes it's a particular trend catapulted into the mainstream through a famous person's wardrobe and picked up by a fast fashion brand, à la Mary Kate Olsen and her leather jackets and oversized bangles. Sometimes it's a product or a brand that garners loyalty because of the trust fans place in a particular public figure. Either way, this influence has so much luster that often it can mask something more sinister, like labor violations in the supply chain or overproduction. When it came to the success of the Air Jordan, for example, it was one of the most publicized supply chain disasters in modern history.

Right before the Air Jordan was released, Nike had moved its production from Japan and the United States to Indonesia, where they could produce their products for significantly lower costs because of sweatshop labor. In 1988, garment workers at Nike contractors Tae Hwa and Pratama Abadi led a strike, claiming they had been paid "training wages," around 85 cents a day, for full-time work. By the '90s, abuse in Nike's supply chain came front and center as awareness of garment worker rights became more mainstream. The 1996 documentary *Behind the Swoosh*, produced by activist Jim Keady, revealed that workers in Indonesian factories making Nike products were paid only $1 a day and were physically and verbally abused, and the conditions in factories were dangerous. That same year, *Life* magazine featured a scathing report revealing forced child labor at Nike factories in Pakistan. A photo on the cover of the issue showed a young boy stitching together a soccer ball with the iconic swoosh logo front and center.[1]

For an article in *Harper's*, Jeffrey Ballinger spoke with a woman in Indonesia making 12 cents per shoe that was selling for $120 a pair. "Her only name is Sadisah, and it's safe to say that she's never heard of Michael Jordan," Ballinger observes. "Nor is she spending her evenings watching him and his Olympic teammates gliding and dunking in primetime from Barcelona. But she *has* heard of the shoe company he endorses—Nike, whose logo can be seen on the shoes and uniforms of many American Olympic athletes this summer."[2] The juxtaposition of the players' success, proudly wearing their Nike gear at an event the whole world was watching, and the image of an appalling paycheck given to a woman who spent hours making their uniforms was something the brand could not escape, though they initially tried.

At first, Nike responded by putting the blame on the factories, claiming that because they didn't own the supply chain, the low wages and forced labor were not their fault. Still, it was a public relations nightmare. In 2004, the *Harvard Business Review* called them "the global poster child for corporate ethical fecklessness."[3] Everyone knew about what was going on, and the deflection to the factories didn't quell the protests and outrage against the company. When CEO Philip Knight spoke at the Stanford Business School in 1997, hundreds of students chanted inside the auditorium: "Hey Philip, off the stage. Pay your workers a living wage," over and over again. Another protest in New York City saw hundreds standing up against sweatshop labor throughout the streets of Manhattan, eventually ending at a Nike store.

By 1998, Nike sales had taken a turn slightly downward, but Knight told the *New York Times* that he "truthfully [did not] think that there has been a material impact on Nike sales by the human rights attacks." Instead, he blamed any sales decline on changing fashion trends and over-expansion into Asia. What's interesting, though, is that in the same year, Nike separated the Jordan brand into its own business and there they continued to turn a profit.

Michael Jordan was and is a beloved figure. He represented greatness in a way that was unheard of. There is nothing wrong with proudly wearing the shoes he created—if anything, that is exactly what fashion is supposed to be. Those shoes were meaningful keepsakes for a lot of people who wear and collect them. They represented something bigger than just a shoe. In 2015, Calvan Fowler, director and writer of the film *Jordan Heads*, described the shoes like this: "It's aspirational," he told *Newsweek*. "It makes people feel special, like when they put these on they're a part of history. It's history that they're documenting. It's history that you can wear on your feet." On a more basic level, Air Jordans are just good sneakers. I have a copper metallic lifted pair that I have been wearing for the last five years.

Still, with the help of mainstream media the stories of Jordan's rising fame and financial success always outweighed the stories of those making the popular sneakers in horrifying conditions. While consumers lined the streets outside of sneakers stores to be part of the culture he created, activists were trying to make the truth of what was going on behind the scenes in the factories known. You can guess which story was the loudest.

In the press, Jordan distanced himself from the issues in a way that helped fans do the same thing. When asked about it at a press conference in 1996, he said he didn't know the "complete" situation. He added, "Why should I? I'm trying to do my job. Hopefully, Nike will do the right thing, whatever that might be."[4]

The sins of a corporation are often ignored because of how quickly the culpability is passed around. There is enough responsibility to go around, and yet no one gets the blame. Was it Michael Jordan's or Kylie Jenner's fault that sweatshops were making the products they had become the face of? Absolutely not. They certainly didn't place the orders or set up any sort of production. At the same time, influencers and public figures are often used to distract from or overshadow public relations crises and nefarious labor practices. To say Nike will do the right thing and move on allowed Jordan's fans to do it too. Nike eventually implemented minimum-wage requirements and more transparency around their factories, but it took almost four years for it to happen.

In that time, the Jordan brand continued to develop, separate from the reputation its parent company had earned. In 1998, the annual report from the company called out the fact that while the rest of the brand had decreased in year-over-year sales by 4 to 17 percent, the Jordan brand increased by about 57 percent.[5] What this says is that despite growing awareness of the brand's toxicity, the influence of Michael Jordan never waned and, in fact, flourished.

At the very end of the report that highlighted the incongruent growth of Jordan, Nike put a section that highlighted the new initiatives in corporate responsibility. Alongside charitable contributions and a promise to encourage diversity, they highlighted six vague points of improvement for their factories, including increasing independent monitoring, raising minimum age, strengthening health and safety standards, expanding education of the workforce, instituting loan programs, and fostering dialogue with workers. At the end of this section, the brand punctuated their promises with a note: "We are serious about these initiatives. We recognize that there is no finish line. Our goal is continuous improvement." The depth of that sentence is refreshingly honest but also sadly accurate in a way they likely didn't intend—the brand is continuing to improve because the problems never really were fixed.

Twenty-two years later, in 2020, with decades of time and technological advancement, another devastating report about Nike's supply chain surfaced. A reporter for the *Washington Post* visited a shoe factory in Qingdao, China, that was making Nike sneakers and alleged that the factory was using forced Uyghur labor. "It resembled a prison, with barbed wire, watchtowers, surveillance cameras and a dedicated police station."[6] They also noted that workers told her that they had not come of their own accord and were not allowed to leave. The biggest story most people heard about, however, was that the Jordan brand made $4.5 billion that year.

The influence Jordan had on Nike customers was remarkable not only because of the amount of money he brought in for the brand, but because of the way in which his influence has continued to evolve in the decades since his first shoe was introduced. When Instagram was launched in October 2010, the creators, Kevin Systrom and Mike Krieger, wanted to create a platform that was image first. It quickly turned into a launchpad for people to monetize their style and gain authority over fashion. Before Instagram, social media existed for mutual connectivity; you had friends on Facebook and MySpace. On Instagram, however, people could be the stars of their own show, making their photos and their perfectly curated outfits a commodity. The exchange was content for a like and follow, not a friendship. The power was placed into influencers' hands, and as their stars rose over the next six years, so did an opportunity for fast fashion brands with a massive marketing budget.

In 2021, Chinese-based ultra-fast fashion brand Shein announced a fashion competition show for young designers on their social media channels. The judges included fashion designers, magazine editors, and major stylists. The feedback from followers on all of the influencers accounts was swift: many criticized the judges for participating in the show and giving even more of a platform to an increasingly problematic brand. In Shein's short history, the company had been accused of stealing designs from independent artists, selling Islamic prayer rugs as decoration, and overproducing garments using sweatshop labor. It was fascinating to see the feedback, because while a few small corners of the internet had been talking about sweatshops and fashion waste, I had never witnessed industry leaders face backlash in this way. The brand's advertising was so blatant that the fans of the people involved couldn't look the other way.

Shein had been called out for ripping off young designers dozens of times prior to the announcement, and by giving a small amount of money back to artists, they were somehow making up for their sins. They have never apologized or paid the people they stole from in the past, and they continue to do it. And as you might have suspected, making clothing that cheap and fast is not without cost to workers. Later in 2021, a report by Timo Kollbrunner at the Public Eye China highlighted the undercover work of a researcher who spoke to Shein employees in Nancun Village, a neighborhood in the Panyu district in China that is almost exclusively Shein factories. The anonymous researcher found that people in the factories were working seventy-five hours per week, well over China's legal maximum of fifty-six hours per week. The researcher also found no emergency exits and remarked that they didn't want to "think about what would happen if a fire broke out there."

It appeared that workers had to clock that many hours in order to make a living wage. "In a good month, he earns up to 10,000 yuan or approximately CHF 1,400 to take home; in bad months it can be only a third of that. There is no over-time premium," the researcher reported. They also note that Shein's orders from the factory for certain styles are generally small, around one hundred to two hundred pieces. Basically, Shein moves with trends fast, and expects them to sell quickly. It makes the work harder for the seamstresses, because they are having to constantly keep up with new patterns and styles.

It would be giving influencers and fashion editors too little credit to assume they didn't know about the potential problems with the brand. There is value in trying to work to change things from the inside, but there is also the risk of legitimizing overproduction and exploitation by giving a stamp of approval to the practices.

For the most part, consumers are savvier than ever before. Still, we are no match for our own psychology. Often the rush we get from clothing and our need to use them to fit in and express our personalities to the outside world makes our propensity for shopping fast fashion even more complex. Not only are we now fighting our impulses to belong and fit in by wearing the latest trends, we are combating our desire to have things that are similar to the ones promoted by celebrities. "We have a basic psychological need. We want to fit in, we want to belong," says fashion psychologist Carolyn Mair. "We want to be our best selves and we want to enhance, so we look to people who we would like to be in their social circle. Social media allows us to do that, you can follow whoever you like and you know you're part of that group in your mind."

And so we follow, and we shop. And sometimes that need

to belong can be so strong that it allows us to justify or ignore behaviors that wouldn't usually fit into our belief systems. "Influence is a very convenient way of belonging to a group that we would never be part of in the real world. Belonging is good for people's mental health, even virtually," Mair goes on to explain. Where this can go wrong is when people can't separate the social media page from reality. They see a new outfit every day on an influencer, and to them it may promote this idea of constantly needing new and more, when in reality most of the items are gifted to the influencer by the brands.

Queue the screeching halt sound, because yes, it's crucial for us all to remember that celebrities and influencers aren't even curating their own wardrobes. From the smallest Instagram boutique to Chanel, brands give away products to get people to post on their Instagram pages. Some disclose what's been gifted and what hasn't, but it's likely that it doesn't even matter—just wearing an item gives a stamp of approval for the loyal follower. We know this as fashion editors, too. In the last ten years, I have written around six hundred stories about what a celebrity is wearing: three hundred words describing, literally head to toe, an outfit on someone like Kendall Jenner or Gigi Hadid. There are some celebrities who I know will garner instant traffic to the website. When I worked at *InStyle*, I jokingly called the website "Jennifer Lopez dot com," because readers would love any outfit she wore, even if it was just jeans and a T-shirt.

We have cognitive bias with the brands and the influencers we love. For the most part we think we know best, so how could we be making a bad choice? In the Nike Air Jordans case, there is sort of a "love is blind" effect. Essentially, people don't see the bad because they are convinced that their love for a brand or a person makes it sound. They proudly wear the iconic Jumpman logo on Air Jordans because they believe that Michael Jordan has good values and therefore Nike is good. "There is a belief that you are correct in your judgment. It's sort of the same way we believe in religion or a political party," Mair says.

This cognitive bias illustrates the power influencers have. If Jordan had felt that he could speak out about the sweatshops in the '90s, maybe it would have pushed the brand to do more about their problems sooner. If influencers and celebrities addressed how gender or racial inequality impact the women making the clothing they're pushing, then perhaps their followers would be more inclined to as well.

Corporations are hard to hold accountable: they're big and have entire marketing teams—including those very celebrities we're talking about—to change the narrative. Imagine how powerful it would be if more celebs spoke out against fast fashion brands' harmful practices and worked with activist groups to change the business. I'm not sure how much impact lesser influencers would have, but powerful celebrities like Kylie Jenner would make a difference if they called out bad behavior. At the very least, they could work with the brands to fix the issues before agreeing to front a campaign for clothing that was made by people in dangerous and exploitative conditions.

Influence is a responsibility, and those who have the luxury of having it on a large scale should use it wisely. No one is saying they have to be a mouthpiece for every issue, but if they are making hundreds of thousands of dollars and the person making the item they're wearing is making $100, that is something to speak on. As consumers, we can also inform and request that the influencers we love push brands to change.

6

The Secret Behind the Logo

THE LATE 1990S AND EARLY 2000S HBO SERIES *Sex and the City* was known for its fashion. Even decades later, articles and websites are dedicated to deciphering the main characters' closets, complete with interviews and hot takes. Of course, like any impressionable millennial who grew up with an unhealthy obsession with New York, I have my favorite pieces among designer Patricia Fields's costuming magnum opus. One piece, in particular, has always stood out to me. It shows up in an episode called "Sex and Another City," in which the four main characters travel from the constraints of crowded New York City restaurants and apartments to find themselves frolicking through wide-open Los Angeles parties filled with porn stars and celebrities. Fields's costuming was often a character in and of itself, used as a metaphor for the larger message the episode was attempting to portray. In this scene, a counterfeit designer purse was added to highlight the characters' issues with letting go of their own moral superiority (read: New York City smokers who tell it like it is) and embracing some harmless duplicity (read: Los Angeles people who talk about who they know and get plastic surgery like it's lunch).

One morning while the group is at breakfast, the character Samantha pulls out a little baguette purse with a Fendi Zucca logo clasp—a design created in 1965 by the late Karl Lagerfeld featuring two opposing Fs that create a square. The main character, Carrie Bradshaw, identifies the purse and yells out an appropriative "No you didn't!"—shocked that her friend had splurged on the purchase. "That's like $3,000," Charlotte, the practical one, says with a gasp. "Or $150," Samantha quips while giving her friends a knowing look. "Fake," she announces before going on to explain that she purchased it from a man selling fake designer bags in the Valley.

She then proceeds to wear her faux-Fendi bag proudly to a party that night at the Playboy mansion. While she's there, though, she misplaces it. Here's where the bag metaphor comes in: as she's searching for her purse, she mistakes a real version that a Playboy bunny is wearing for her own. She grabs the little gold bag from under the alleged culprit's arm and yells, "It's mine!" As Hugh Heffner walks over playing himself, Samantha looks at him and desperately pleads, "Just look, you'll see 'Made in China' on the inside," she tells him. When the bunny flips the bag inside out, she reveals that hers was in fact "Made in Italy." She had the real thing. Samantha is immediately called out and shamed for having a fake bag. The embarrassment instantly forces her to rethink her position, and at that moment, the lesson of the whole episode becomes clear.

The reason I've always found the designer bag allegory so fascinating is that it never addresses the most interesting piece of what makes a fake bag so bad. Is it because it's made in China? China and almost every other major manufacturing country have both incredibly well-run factories *and* sweatshops. Is it because you're being deceptive about how much you spent on it? As Samantha said, it looks exactly the same, so what's the problem? What does owning a fake bag actually say about her?

Counterfeiting production happens all around the world, but for the sake of this story, let's say it was produced in Italy, where Fendi is headquartered. Factories that make fake fashion goods have been linked to forced labor of migrants and refugees, including children. In 2008, the book *Gomorrah* by

Roberto Saviano details how the Italian criminal organization known as the Camorra did exactly this with luxury fashion. As he explains it, the factories hire organized crime leaders around the country to bring in migrant workers who are paid $3 or less an hour for fourteen-hour days.[1]

And the reason that the fakes are so good, Saviano says, is that often the people making them were formerly employed making the real thing. "The same hands that once worked under the table for the big labels now work for the clans. . . . Which means that the clothes made by the clans aren't typical counterfeit goods . . . but rather a sort of true fake," he writes. "All that's missing is the final step: the brand name, the official authorization from the motherhouse."

Not all counterfeit bags are made this way, and there are plenty of people who will say that these stories are overblown. But even if it's one factory recruiting vulnerable people and placing them in conditions that are considered modern slavery just to make a fake Fendi bag, that's reason enough to try and change the system.

On the buyer side, there is deception as well, because not everyone is a willing customer. Often people purchasing fake designer pieces don't even realize they're doing it. As production becomes digitized, it's easier for these proprietary designs to get into the hands of organized counterfeiting rings, and sometimes even authenticators can't tell the difference. It happened to me in 2016, right before I went on my first-ever assignment for *Vogue*. I was asked to attend a fancy ball in Manhattan and write about the famous people there, the atmosphere, and any gossip. I felt like a total imposter, terrified and feeling like

I tricked them into letting me write this story. I went to my closet to find something to wear to this event, and I had nothing. My job waitressing didn't afford me a closet that screamed "Vogue"; instead, it was lined with Salvation Army and Urban Outfitters. I immediately went to eBay to search for the perfect black jumpsuit. I wanted it to have a tight bodice with wide legs, so it was fancy enough for an event, but loose enough that I could move around for my reporting, which, apparently, I thought required agility. I typed in the descriptors, and voilà, the perfect Phillip Lim jumpsuit popped up. And better yet, it was only $40 for the starting bid. Immediately, I plugged in an offer for $43.50 and won.

Two days later and a day before the event, my jumpsuit arrived, pumping confidence into my veins that I didn't have in the week leading up to this moment. When I opened the box, however, something was off. It certainly looked like the black jumpsuit I'd ordered, but the material felt rough. There were a few strings on the top, and the tag was sewn a little sideways. At first, I told myself this was normal because the clothing had been worn before, and sometimes resale is inaccurately listed as new to get it to sell. I ran to my bathroom to try it on, pulling the jumpsuit over my butt, zipping it up, ready to imagine myself as the new, serious fashion reporter I had become. When I looked in the mirror, though, I realized the legs were slightly different lengths. That didn't make any sense for a designer outfit.

I unzipped it and looked again at the cockeyed tag that read "Phillip Lim" and realized I had bought a fake. When I tried to return the item, the eBay store had already been taken down and there was no one I could complain to. The four hours of work that it took me to pay for that outfit had been flushed down the toilet, and a lump of fabric mocked me with its presence. I still went to the party, of course, I just wore something I bought at H&M—and I felt mostly fine. The room was dark and there were Cirque du Soleil acrobats dangling from the ceiling. Waiters asked me if I wanted a piece of meat on a fancy little stick and others offered me cocktails. I mingled, I got my interviews, took notes, and that was it. No one gave a shit about my outfit. The loss for me was the $50 I spent and the fact that the outfit was going to go to waste.

Since then, the risk of accidental counterfeit purchases has increased. Resale apps make it easier for a counterfeit to slip through as the real thing. There are hundreds of accounts from people who spent thousands on designer pieces from websites like eBay or the RealReal only to have the same experience I did when they arrived. Some websites have even begun creating partnerships with the brands so that the authentication process is more secure.

For designers, the damage is to their brand integrity and to their intellectual property; both issues that are difficult to defend. In 2016, designer Alexander Wang won a lawsuit against fifty-six counterfeit websites bearing domain names close to his, selling fake versions of his shoes, clothing, and bags. He was awarded $90 million, and the websites were shut down. It was a win for the integrity of the brand, but not necessarily something that would change the system in which counterfeiting operates, because a lawsuit doesn't address labor problems or even financial issues.

"I think the biggest brands make these lawsuits part of a routine civil enforcement of their brand," explains the Fashion Law founder Julie Zerbo. They file so many of these cases against thousands of websites, and they don't actually know who the defendants are. "They identify them by website, or in some cases by identifying them by Amazon seller name or social media handle." She goes on to say that the defendants are usually several steps ahead of the brand and rarely show up to court because they are not even within the jurisdiction. For example, if Alexander Wang filed his lawsuit in New York State and the accused was just a website in China, the person or people he was suing were likely unknown to him. Mostly, the result is simply that the site is closed and moved elsewhere. If anything, it's usually the middleman, the person selling the product on the street, who gets in trouble.

In 2021, the U.S. attorney's office for the Eastern District of New York released a press release saying they had indicted four defendants who participated in a $130 million scheme to sell fake UGGs, Air Jordans, and Timberland boots. The defendants allegedly imported generic goods from China and brought them to a warehouse in Queens, where logos and trademarks from the brands they copied were applied. The goods were then sold to wholesalers. "As alleged, the defendants trafficked counterfeit merchandise they fraudulently branded as genuine to pass off to purchasers in the United States at a purported retail value of more than $130 million," stated Acting United States Attorney Jacquelin Kasulis.[2] They went on to say that the office is committed to "holding defendants accountable for their greed." The release cites the "detrimental impact" fake goods have on the economy.

Once again, it seems like the investigation completely ignored that fact due to insufficient transparency in the supply chain for counterfeit items, and never once mentioned that those fake UGG boots probably had ties to modern slavery. It's good that designers are working to end counterfeiting to protect themselves, but the issue is that human rights violations of workers who likely made the products are never investigated, and rarely even addressed.

There is a myth that because something is designer it's made ethically or even by hand. For thousands of dollars a bag or dress, you would think that would be the case. But pricing is not necessarily based on labor, especially when it comes to entry items like a sandal or a pair of designer sunglasses. KnowTheChain, a benchmarking tool that can be used by companies and investors as a resource to address forced labor in their global supply chain, published a report in 2020 that found that luxury brands had higher risks than mid-level brands of modern slavery in their supply chain because they deem information on their supply chain proprietary. "Where luxury brands are shying away from is just transparency," former KnowTheChain director Felicitas Weber told me one day in a Zoom call. She said it's a contentious issue for labor rights activists, because the luxury brands will claim the sourcing is proprietary but will tell customers that products and materials mainly come from France or Italy. The problem is that it's not the truth. The leather may be assembled in Italy, but it may come from India and not be marked that way. And just because a product is made in Italy doesn't mean the workers aren't at risk.

When Weber and I spoke, I found myself feeling surprised. It's not that I didn't think luxury brands were problematic—if anything, I find them to be annoyingly sanctimonious. They are contributing to fashion waste and unstoppable trend cycles just as much as any other brand, and yet we hold them to a different standard. What stood out to me was that according to KnowTheChain's findings, some of the most prestigious and expensive brands in the world, like Hermès, scored much lower on a transparency index than fast fashion brands.

Scoring low doesn't mean that they are definitely using forced labor, but to me it says that their branding and their exclusivity is more important than making sure the workers throughout the supply chain are taken care of. Because even if they think they are better than other brands, there is no way to prove that without being fully transparent in their supply chain, from materials to assembly.

Take the "Made in Italy" logo that was so pridefully shown off on the real Fendi bag in that episode of *Sex in the City*, for instance. It was supposed to symbolize old-school leather-working and well-paid craftsmanship passed down through the decades. But while it could certainly be expertly made, it doesn't mean it's some old Italian man working in his grandfather's factory being paid a living wage. In Tuscany, for example, the factories that make clothing and accessories are staffed by an estimated fifty thousand Chinese migrants, many of whom work in sweatshops, creating goods for luxury brands.

In 2019, a man named Vincenzo Capezzuto was placed under house arrest on charges of "illegal employment and abduction." He was the head of Moreno Srl in Naples, which has made bags and shoes for Fendi, Saint Laurent, and Armani. When authorities searched his workshop, they found around fifty migrant workers, including pregnant women and teenagers, hiding behind rolls of leather and piles of shoes and bags. The brands either denied or neglected to comment on the matter. The other part of the murky supply chain problems in luxury is that leathers are assembled in Italy, but often come from South America, Bolivia, South Sudan, Brazil, Niger, or Paraguay— where exploitation on factory farms is a known issue.

It sounds bleak, but it all leads me to one trend in fashion that perpetuates both the problems in counterfeiting and the problems in luxury that I think we can all have a hand in changing: logomania. I'm not just talking about wearing head-to-toe logos, but also the premium so many people place on those logos. It's the fact that we think having something expensive makes us better. And that we feel the need to let our clothing do the talking through a brand name and not our own personal style.

The very idea of using a symbol to show off our status is centuries old but has been retrofitted to our modern age in fashion. A family crest used to be the symbol you would wear or fly to highlight your legacy and boast about your achievements within society. Centuries later, in the 1980s, people began to use brand logos to show off their taste and wealth. "The symbolism associated with Gucci, for example, is actually symbolism transference," legendary Harlem couturier Dapper Dan said when speaking with the *New York Times*. "When I was growing up, if you had diamonds and furs, that gave you clout. So, when the big fashion brands began to come out, I noticed how people gravitated toward them, and that what identified these brands was their logo. I incorporated that symbol in a way that represented fashion as I see it. This symbol, when it's incorporated in fashion in a certain way and reflected through a certain culture, has the same impact as diamonds and furs."[3]

This astute observation highlights how a brand logo can incorporate both the status that a diamond can give and the sense of community that comes with a crest. This is why in the '90s, the logo itself became the look. The economy was thriving, and wearing logos from luxury brands was a sartorial flex of that moment in time. It was less about excess and more about highlighting affluence.

A black Chanel bag might indicate both someone who has enough money to spend $5,000 on a purse, and someone who cares about classic style. Tommy Hilfiger wearers were hip and into cultural moments and trends. The all-American brand may have had a slightly more affordable price tag than some brands, but the decade's biggest stars—Britney Spears, En Vogue, Destiny's Child, and even Usher—wore it, and it meant something to copy that style. The Fendi logo that Samantha so desperately wanted to wear while she was in Los Angeles was a favorite of top supermodels, like Kate Moss and Christy Turlington. Wearing it meant there was a certain chicness and edginess to your style.

Logomania was a concept that anyone watching *Sex and the City* could understand. The show itself promoted it throughout its entire six-season run. Certain handbag trends, like the Dior saddlebag that featured the brand's iconic D all over the fabric, were even attributed to the characters. Logo bags were part of their fashion prowess. They knew about and had the latest things, and it was part of who they were. A fake bag was out of character, but the idea was that they wanted the logo to show off their class status. I have been gifted vintage Chanel and vintage Fendi by resale websites. They are certainly well crafted, with leather that is undeniably high quality. But I would be lying if I said that walking around with a little red Chanel bag, emblazoned with the iconic crossed C logo didn't make me feel like I was part of a different stratum of society.

The 2008 recession may have been the catalyst for a brief moment when it became gauche to wear head-to-toe Fendi. I think the reality was that the moment for the trend had expired, but having a logo bag has never truly gone out of style, because the premium we put on those little symbols is almost untouchable.

Even more so, logos came back in 2019, and never went away again during the economic downturn of 2020. The fashion industry perpetuates class hierarchy through logomania. If everyone could have the same things, there would be no aspiration—which is what keeps these brands in business. If logos had no power, counterfeiting would be impacted at least in a small way. What does a fake Fendi bag mean without the look of the brand's signature Zucca clasp—the one that signals the bag's worth?

Realistically, the power that comes from a brand logo or proprietary design will never go away. It's probably a little too late to change the capitalistic mindset that got us to a place where we bow at the altar of a Gucci logo. But maybe, if we take a page from the anti-fur movement, it could be tarnished enough to force change. Since the earliest days of luxury fashion, mink, chinchilla, and fox furs were used in almost every winter collection. Furs were a sign of wealth and class in the same way a diamond is now. But over the decades and especially in the 1990s, animal rights activist groups like PETA used guerilla tactics like crashing fashion shows and pouring fake blood on attendees who were wearing fur.

In 2002, PETA crashed the Victoria's Secret fashion show, jumping onto the runway with a sign that read "Gisele: Fur Scam." It was a moment that never made the broadcast but was talked about for years after. Even the models were so jolted by it that it changed their relationship with brands that sold fur. "Suddenly it dawned on me," supermodel Gisele Bündchen told *Vogue* fifteen years later.[4] "I was on the hamster wheel: I'm just going to go out there and be a good girl and do what my agent tells me to do. What do I know? It wasn't until that shock— it stopped me in my tracks. They sent me all these videos. I wasn't aware of what was happening, and I was devastated. So, I said, 'Listen, I'm not doing fur campaigns.' It put me in the driver's seat, finally. The universe comes to you and says, 'Hello, maybe you should notice this.' You need to be responsible for the choices you make."

For over two decades, Gisele was one of the most sought-after, highest-paid models in the world. Her experience being the focal point of a campaign led by activists pushed her to change. I wouldn't doubt more models followed her lead, because while

PETA's tactics have always been divisive, in this case they worked. By 2018, Gucci, Coach, Versace, Burberry, Armani, Ralph Lauren, Tommy Hilfiger, Michael Kors, Vivienne Westwood, Prada, Chanel, and more had removed all products with fur from their collections, although it should be noted that leather is still very much part of their sourced material.

If we applied the same level of public denouncement and demonization to the violation of human rights, then perhaps we could help force the brands to do more. One of PETA's most successful campaigns featured celebrities like Pamela Anderson, Eva Mendes, Olivia Munn, and others who would pose naked with the tagline "I'd rather go naked than wear fur." After twenty years of the campaign, the organization eventually declared victory in 2020 and retired their celebrity marketing altogether. I am in no way comparing the two issues, I am simply illustrating what can work when we make it wrong to buy into something harmful. Imagine the equivalent energy toward brands that abuse and exploit their workers. The awareness of how these issues are caused by more than just fast fashion would increase immensely.

On the counterfeiting side, though, it's more difficult. "The most obvious answer to taking legal action comes in the form of the various modern slavery laws that exist," says Zerbo when I ask her what she thinks could be done. "If they can show that the products are, in fact, created in circumstances that violate laws, then technically that could be a way in." She adds that she has never seen a brand go that route, and, typically, the only way that legal action is happening is through U.S. customs when they are able to stop the products from getting through the

border. That's a Band-Aid, though, and it just makes the coun-
terfeiters more careful and possibly even less visible than they
were before. By the time the products reach a port, the damage
has already been done. People have already made the products
in poor conditions and intellectual property has already been
stolen. The problem is that it's underground, making it harder
to stop at the source.

As long as the trends continue to shift, so will the desire for
cheaper alternatives. If you've ever walked through a counterfeit market in New York City or Seoul, it feels like the demand
will never let up.

Still, there has to be a solution, and it should probably come
from the people who are impacted the most. "Whenever you
have an IT problem, you go to an IT person; when you want
bread, you go to a baker; but when you want to fix labor issues,
nobody goes to workers," Weber says. It's a really simple way
to highlight the fact that any solution to stop counterfeiting is
often found in a courtroom with people who were the very last
to know. The counterfeiting world can be dangerous for workers, and those coming forward could be risking their lives, but
no one understands the situation better than someone who
has been there.

Outside of the obvious similarities in logos and designs, the
luxury and counterfeiting world have something else in common: the secrecy around how exactly that bag or top ended
up at its final destination before you bought it. In some ways,
this has value for the brands, because in fashion, gatekeeping
certain elements of the final product is where the allure comes
from. But as it stands now, the charm that mystery can bring to

a brand is far less valuable than the justice transparency could bring to people in the supply chain. It's almost surprising that the luxury brands wouldn't want to make that distinction, especially when one of the reasons people buy counterfeits is because they look exactly the same. The real difference is how they're made. As consumers we should know exactly what that means, and we should demand that those workers have a safe way to tell us.

7

Green Is the New Black

Imagine a world where fast fashion brands put out sustainable collections, with tops made of recycled fabric and shoes that have been produced using plastic bottles. This is a world where brands also post about their standards at the factories, including zero tolerance for child labor and rigorous compliance to laws regulating minimum wage and workplace safety. These brands embrace circularity, implementing recycling and buyback programs where customers can return their worn pieces instead of throwing them into a landfill. Sounds amazing, right?

The world we just imagined already exists. It exists right now all over the internet and across fast fashion brands. Campaigns touting a commitment to sustainability using young activists as a way to reach a new generation of consumers who care about style and climate change can be found at almost every major fashion brand. If you google "sustainable fashion," it's likely that some brands that are making two collections a week will pop up in that search. Most of them are using a stealthy marketing technique commonly known as greenwashing. This strategy has been used by brands of all types for decades to make it appear that they align with ethical standards when really, they haven't made that many changes.

The term *greenwashing* was coined in the mid-1980s by environmentalist Jay Westervelt. He was on a research trip to Samoa when he stopped in Fiji to surf. After he was finished riding a piece of foam through the waves off a beautiful island, he reportedly broke into a hotel to steal a towel. It was there that he saw a small card attached to the pile asking patrons to pick up their towels and reuse them in order to reduce ecological damage. The card read: "Save Our Planet: Every day, millions of gallons of water are used to wash towels that have only been used once. You make the choice: A towel on the rack means, 'I will use again.' A towel on the floor means, 'Please replace.' Thank you for helping us conserve the Earth's vital resources." It was an absurd concept, he felt, especially from a hotel chain that was rapidly expanding on the islands, using up natural resources and encouraging more travelers to visit.

Westervelt recalled the incident in an interview with *The Guardian* thirty years later, saying, "I finally wrote something like, 'It all comes out in the greenwash.' A guy in the class with me worked for a literary magazine and had me write an essay about it." The concept took off from there. Throughout the '90s, awareness of greenwashing grew but the practice just got sneakier across a range of different industries. As consumers became more conscious of environmental concerns around consumption, so did the brands—but they capitalized on it. Instead of fixing the issues by changing materials or the number of products they sell, they incorporated only minor fixes like recycling labels or bins, even though much of what goes into them can't actually be reused. Some brands were even more literal with greenwashing by adding green logos to signify that their products were organic or environmentally friendly when in actuality, they were only marginally more sustainable.

Among fashion consumers, however, awareness of how disposable our clothing has become was beginning to take hold. In the mid-2000s, reports began to surface about landfills piled to the top with discarded clothing made from cheap materials. Between 1990 and 2010, the amount of textile waste in landfills more than doubled. It became clear that this waste was detrimental to the environment when studies showed how materials like the plastic and petroleum found in cheap clothing would end up in groundwater.

As a result of the growing concern about fashion's sustainability problems, H&M launched the "Conscious Collection" in 2010. It was a small line of basics made partially with recycled materials like Tencel—rayon made from reused pulp—and organic cotton. At the time it was a big deal. No other fast fashion brand was even trying to combat issues with sustainability, and H&M was finally, seemingly, taking a stand. I was still in college at the time, so while I would have loved to buy something recycled, I still wanted trendy pieces, and the collection was not that at all. The run was more of the classic "eco" look with all white and beige items, loose fits and maxi skirts—a real cliché of the classic vegan bohemian and certainly not the vibe for the average customer. Still, the line made it into hundreds of stores, and people praised the brand for stepping up when others wouldn't. Two years later, they took it a step further and introduced influencers into the mix when they released an "exclusive" line. These more dressed-up items were worn on red carpets by celebrities like Michelle Williams, Amanda Seyfried, and others.

At the BAFTAs, Williams, looking elegant in a gold strapless top and black skirt, stood among her fellow celebrities and blended right in. Every single headline read something to the effect of, "Can You BELIEVE Michelle Williams Is Wearing H&M on the RED CARPET!" It was pretty extraordinary, given the premiums we place on high fashion luxury versus trendy or contemporary, and it did exactly what the brand needed: it gave H&M attention for doing something—anything—about the perceived problems in fashion. It also pushed forward the narrative that what they were doing would be the change we needed in order to democratize sustainability. Without a closer look at what was really going on behind the scenes, and with the help of some trustworthy famous faces, most people would peg H&M as a leader in sustainability in the 2010s.

It also helped that alongside the exclusive collection release the brand posted a "conscious report," which touted all of the amazing things they were doing to be more ethical. "74% of our managers are women," the report read in a little blue bubble. "570,821 workers in Bangladesh have been educated about their rights since 2008," read a small bullet point on another page.[1] There were charts showing the increase in water-based soles on the shoes they sell, and others that used phrases like "value chain impact." It was filled with hedging on promises, using qualifiers that claimed things would be better by a specific date in the future, or using big bold percentages alongside a hopeful promise about change.

The blatant marketing of it all was backed up by an interview Helena Helmersson, head of sustainability for H&M, gave to *The Guardian*.[2] "A lot of people ask for guarantees: 'Can you guarantee labor conditions? Can you guarantee zero chemicals?'" she explained to the interviewer. Responding to the questions, she said: "Of course, we cannot when we're such a huge company operating in very challenging conditions. What I can say is that we do the very best we can with a lot of resources and a clear direction of what we're supposed to do. We're working really hard." Why, then, were they selling their customers on something conscious when they could not, in fact, promise or guarantee, as she put it, that it would be?

What's more—if they were selling those items, why couldn't they guarantee proper labor conditions or zero harmful chemicals? No one was forcing companies to make new clothing. H&M could have downsized production, gotten total control of the supply chain, and been able to make those guarantees. It was never about sweeping change. All of those numbers and words were marketable, and that was the most important piece. That year, statistics about fashion's impact on the planet and the garment workers were entering the global consciousness, and some brands saw an opportunity to fill a hole in the market. As customers, we want to have our cake and eat it too. We want to shop all the time and buy new clothing. And we also want to do less harm. Fast fashion sustainability lets us feel like we can do both, when the reality is, that's not a possibility. Cost is a source of contention for people who say they want to shop sustainably and ethically but don't feel that it is financially viable.

While thrifting is certainly an option, there are still problems within that. For starters, secondhand clothing has become a trend in itself, driving up prices so that they are often the same as what's being sold new. And giving money to Salvation Army or Goodwill, where things are often the most affordable, is buying into another labor issue altogether. Both of these companies hire people with disabilities or who are in recovery and, through a loophole in the laws, pay them below minimum wage for the same work as other employees.

Outside of thrifting and the issues that come with it, there is truth to the assumption that in order to shop well you have to spend more, but that notion is complex and needs to be broken down. If we're looking at it simply, better-sourced materials that have less chemicals and are produced by farmers making living wages will add cost to the product. Paying the garment workers assembling the clothing a fair wage and guaranteeing safe conditions in factories means the product is going to cost more. If we want our packaging to be made from recycled materials, that will also, unfortunately, cost more. It's an entire system that's built to make us choose to do wrong.

For brands that have built entire business models on cheaper prices, the question is: Will customers spend more for clothes made by people making a living wage, working legal hours, in humane conditions? There is a good example of how changes can be made in a way that includes the customer.

"It happened in 2015 and I had been on a very sort of particular trajectory with the brand," designer Mara Hoffman told me one day during the height of the global pandemic. We were on Zoom, which had quickly become the norm for seeing people during that winter. We talked about how weird fashion felt in that moment. We had all these clothes and no place to wear them. As a designer it was even more challenging for her. She felt a responsibility to her brand and her employees, but she also felt a burden of not wanting to continue making clothing the same way when everything had changed so much that year. Her customers didn't necessarily want new clothes, and she had to make hard decisions to stay afloat.

So, Hoffman stopped. She sent out an email, right around

Fashion Week, explaining that she would be skipping that season and she would put out new clothing only when it made sense for her and her customers. She also announced a circularity program: she would essentially buy back clothing she sold and remake it into something new. It was exciting to see someone actually make these choices, which are a huge risk but a rewarding one if it works.

The thing is, Hoffman's eponymous brand wasn't always like this. She was going about the fashion business in the traditional way. She was making exciting collections every season and showing them at Fashion Week. Hoffman even appeared on an episode of the MTV reality show *The City* (a spinoff of the aughts hit *The Hills*) during Miami Swim Week. If you haven't seen either of those shows and love chaotic fashion-adjacent television, I highly recommend going back and watching. It is a prime example of the way independent designers are taught to get their footing. You make clothing, and you make clothing, and you make clothing until someone notices you, and then you keep doing more and bigger. But there was a point for Hoffman where she couldn't do it anymore.

"We had really established a groove and a niche for what we were doing and a really particular aesthetic around what the brand was. The sales were really picking up. We were in tons of department stores. However, in the few years leading up to that I had come into a different level of awareness around the industry itself and what was happening," Hoffman explained. So, at the height of her success, she made a tough decision, one that she wasn't even sure was the right one to make at the time. She decided that she couldn't just talk about wanting to be sustainable while making only incremental moves; she needed to change her entire business model. "We haven't pioneered anything. We definitely, in my opinion, came too late. When we made the change, I felt immense levels of discomfort about what I was doing as a brand. I began to wish that we weren't part of a really shitty industry that was creating so much waste. My son is three years old now, my legacy to him will be that I have piles of shit with my name sewn in with the back label on it and for what? For what?" she asked. It was an interesting way to think about clothing waste from someone who looks at garments as their art. What does clothing become when it ends up in the trash?

Though she admits she has a long way to go to become even more equitable, in the last few years, Hoffman has become something of a poster child for how brands can pivot. She maintains the same aesthetic she always had, with bright patterns on expertly designed dresses. Her silhouettes are unmistakable, structured bodices with voluminous sleeves that are playful but not so much that you would be uncomfortable. But she makes less, uses carefully curated fabrics, and has a very close relationship with her suppliers to make sure all of her garment workers are being paid minimum wage. As we discussed, it's not something she wants a pat on the back for because it's what she *should* be doing. It's what everyone should be doing. But it is so rare for someone to set aside their own ego and success in order to do the right thing that when it happens, it feels tectonic. Comfort and money are intoxicating, and making big changes kills that buzz. Brands will lose customers and sales. They'll also have to work harder to find suitable materials and factories. It's not an easy transition. That's part of why so many brands will do the least amount of work needed to satisfy the cultural push toward sustainability.

Hoffman is interesting to me because she wanted to make a change and so she did. That simple. She was done contributing to the "shitty" parts of the industry and so she didn't anymore. She's still working on making things better and more sustainable (there is no such thing as sustainable new clothing, she reminded me), but she has made the brand something of a beacon for other small designers who want to make a foray into ethical fashion.

I mention Hoffman in the context of greenwashing because I think it's important to understand the difference between actually evolving your brand to be something that causes less harm and making false promises so that you can send out a press release. With a laugh and a wince, Hoffman told me that marketing her efforts feel "cringey." Doing some big campaign around it is not only out of her budget, it's often precarious, because *you're supposed to be sustainable.* You're supposed to pay your workers. It shouldn't be something that even needs to be marketed. And that makes the greenwashing at fast fashion brands so sinister. Why does it have to be splashed on a billboard when it's what you should have been doing all along?

It's still so rare for brands to be making real efforts to change that the ones who are have to let customers know. Then, really, it's on us to decipher whether the information we're getting about the brand is true. This type of marketing is what Patagonia has perfected over the last several decades. The brand is arguably one of the most recognizable corporations with or without their efforts around climate change and global impact. In the 1980s, Patagonia's colorful fleece pullovers were a cross-generational staple, and the popularity of that jacket made them one of the top outerwear brands in the world. By the '90s though, they had overexpanded, leading them to near bankruptcy. It was then that they vowed to make a last-ditch effort to become as sustainable as possible, honing in on a mission and hoping customers would follow along.

Patagonia became one of the first fashion brands to implement a lifetime repair policy on its clothing. They switched materials to make the garments more durable and began working with Fair Trade for their cotton sourcing. Marketing this change could have come across as disingenuous, but the way they did was the antithesis to the greenwash. In 2001, they took out a now-infamous ad in the *New York Times* that read, "Don't buy this jacket," alongside a huge image of the pullover fleece. It was placed right around Black Friday, a holiday built on overconsumption, as a way to tell customers to think twice before they purchase. Still, sales increased by approximately 30 percent in the nine months following the publication of the ad. If we take the copy at face value, it proved that even seemingly radical stances against capitalistic practices that contribute to environmental problems are marketable. As such, it's a strategy that most brands would want to tap into.

Continuing the success of H&M's Conscious Collection (which is still in production today), in 2021 the company launched another campaign around sustainability, but this time it was a more general promotion of the brand. In the ads, young activists like Mari Copeny (aka Little Miss Flint), Elijah Lee, and Brandon Baker all stand wearing H&M clothing with slogans like "you're never too young to be a role model." In the window displays at the stores, the brand paid homage to climate strikes by putting fake protest posters that said, "ECO-WARRIOR AND CLIMATE CRUSADER," "THE FUTURE BELONGS TO THOSE WHO WILL LIVE IT," and "IT ALL STARTS WITH PLANTING A SEED." The corporatization of the youth climate movement in a fast fashion ad campaign felt like gaslighting. It's important that these activists are given a platform, and H&M has a massive one. I don't blame them or their guardians for choosing to work with the brand to promote climate justice. But when the critical problems are not being met with actual solutions it's difficult not to see the sinister side of this kind of campaign.

In England, activist Tolmeia Gregory used the same tactic H&M was using as a marketing tool against the campaign itself. She even went so far as to stage a protest in the window displays at the stores. In an image shared on social media, Gregory is sitting in the window with her legs crossed. She's wearing a green blazer over a black shirt that says "fuck H&M." In other images, she's staring into the camera holding up her middle finger, and in others she holds up signs of her own. "96% of H&M's green claims ignore the EU commission," says the sign she's holding. It was referring to H&M's promises to comply to the European Union's standards for textile and fashion companies. Another one of her signs simply says, "Justice for Jeyasre," the garment worker who was killed at a factory making H&M clothing in 2020.

The juxtaposition of Gregory's signs and the ones created for the ads was one of the best displays of the layered issues that come into play when a company uses change as a selling point, while avoiding a fundamental overhaul of their wasteful practices. I don't highlight H&M so often because I have a bone to pick—but rather because I genuinely think the brand could be a catalyst if they actually made the changes they promised. In June 2021, the Changing Markets "Synthetic Anonymous Report" found that 72 percent of H&M's Conscious Collection was made from synthetic materials. Competitors like Zara and ASOS, which also have sustainable sub-brands, scored significantly better (45 and 57 percent synthetic, respectively), but interestingly H&M's collection gets the most press. The problem, as always, is that the brands making small incremental changes aren't moving fast enough for the lives being impacted right now. It didn't save Jeyasre and it won't fix the amount of clothing ending up in landfills and warehouses around the world.

Fashion is also guilty of taking greenwashing to a new level, where it's not just about recycling or using organic fabrics, but also using messaging to cover up other social-responsibility violations like the use of sweatshops. Many activists have begun to use the term *bluewashing*, which started to gain popularity after CEOs signed the United Nations Global Impact Initiative and then failed to follow through with the standards. *Blue* was a reference to the UN logo, which many were able to use to tout responsibility and transparency without actually meeting goals. Now *bluewashing* is used as a blanket term for companies that use misleading tactics to lead consumers to believe that they are more ethical than they are.

An example in fashion might be a brand like Everlane, which uses the fact that they pay the minimum wage at their factories around the globe as a core pillar in their marketing. The brand says that they have "radical transparency," but what they mean by that is that they tell customers why products cost what they do, breaking down labor and material costs at checkout. They also have an ethical promise to pay legal wages. The problem is that just because it's legal doesn't mean that it equates to a living wage.

On the "about" page of the Everlane website, the brand displays photos of their workers in the factories where they sew the clothing, but what about those making the raw materials used? It's not radical to simply trace one piece of a very large supply chain.

Additionally, in 2020 in the midst of the pandemic, employees at Everlane's retail stores in the United States claimed that management was trying to prevent them from forming a union. While the brand claimed that they had fired workers because of a loss of revenue, workers say it was a union-busting tactic that they had been using for months. The workers went on to file an unfair labor practice charge with the National Labor Relations Board, but eventually dropped it. In August of that same year, the union effort's Twitter account said that Everlane had "concocted a narrative" about downsizing prior to unionizing efforts. They went on to say, "Everlane is far from being absolved. From the start, our job was created as a part-time position to avoid giving benefits, to overwork and underpay us, to exploit our labor in the name of 'ethical fashion.' When we asked for ethical treatment ourselves, we were disposed of." It's why claims of transparency are so capricious and have to be viewed through a skeptical lens.

In 2019, *New York Times* reporters Elizabeth Paton and Sapna Maheshwari wrote that H&M was among the most transparent brands in fashion. On its website, H&M had listed its suppliers, all of which had signed the Bangladesh Accord on Fire and Building Safety, a legally binding agreement ensuring building safety in Bangladesh in the wake of the Rana Plaza collapse. However, Paton and Maheshwari point out that listing suppliers and making commitments is only the first step and in no way guarantees a safer environment for employees—even when there are audits. Especially when H&M refuses to budge on cost with these factories. In many of the contracts the brand has with factories, labor cost was not negotiable, and when overtime is required to finish orders on time, the workers don't see any more pay.

Lutful Matin, a Dhaka factory owner, explained how it works in the *New York Times*: "Brands like H&M offer training, help union members establish themselves in my factory and guide us on investing in the business, which are all very good and important things," he said. "But then their buying teams still drive down order values and I feel such pressure." There is no reward for having better standards in your factory, he claimed. Often his competitors continue to have subpar standards, making their prices lower, and brands will contract with them instead. "Sometimes I don't know how easy it will be to survive," he finished.[3]

As customers, we're told that "supply chain transparency" is a metric for how ethical a brand is. Why wouldn't we think that's all there is to it? If a brand says that they know exactly where the clothing is being made, and they are telling us where that is, it's reasonable that customers would think that the factory has been vetted. But that's not always the case. Felicitas Weber, of KnowTheChain, brought up the point that maybe the problem isn't just knowing which factories are making our clothing, but why there is so much subcontracting in the first place. If you are subcontracting your manufacturing to a third party, which is then outsourcing some of that work to another factory that may not have the same standards as the one that is adhering to the policies set forth by the brand, then the same risk is there. This is where we've hit a wall in the ethical fashion movement.

The benchmarks we've set allow the fashion industry to do the very least, while creating massive amounts of waste using unsustainable materials and dyes—all while underpaying and mistreating workers. The brands use our advocacy against us by putting out advertisements that say they are auditing their factories and only working with the ones adhering to the rules. Meanwhile, those factories are subcontracting work to sweatshops. They get to say they are becoming more sustainable with organic fabrics, while they are still creating new collections once a week, many with synthetic fibers that will end up in landfills and in our water.

As consumers, we can only know what we are told, and that's why greenwashing needs policy to combat misleading advertising. Brands have invited us into the conversation about ethical clothing, and so they should be held legally liable for the claims they make—it shouldn't be up to the customer to police them. It should be up to the government to make sure that they are keeping citizens safe, whether it's the employees or those of us purchasing the clothing.

Without incentive, most brands won't do the right thing. There's simply not as much money in actually following through on being transparent or doing what's best for the environment. They would need to make less and admit their failures—not exactly the recipe for success that we've all been taught. So they need to be forced to do so.

In December 2021, a group of people sued New Balance, a brand known for sneakers and athleticwear, in a Massachusetts district court for their use of "Made in the USA" on most of their products and marketing. The problem was that up to 30 percent of their offerings are made internationally, and the soles of their sneakers are made in China. It's neither ethical nor unethical to make clothing outside of the United States. As we've learned, you can have sweatshops and overproduction anywhere around the world. New Balance was using "Made in America" to place a premium on the type of product by suggesting that it was made in a more ethical manner and was of higher quality because it was made in the United States. The Federal Trade Commission has laws that prohibit misleading marketing, and if the case is successful, it could set a precedent for how these types of claims are made. Without consequence, there will be no transparency from brands. Not everyone has the means to sue a major corporation, but the threat of action could make changes in a major way.

8

Outside the Factory

In Indonesia, about seven hours from the capital city of Jakarta, there is a small village called Gesikharjo, a fishing port that sits in the Tuban district of East Java. It's here that batik, a traditional Indonesian fabrication technique, lives on. Batik is done by carefully placing small amounts of hot wax onto fabric in order to block out small patterns. Once the wax is applied and cooled, everything is dyed multiple times with different colors. After the wax is removed, what's left are gorgeous handmade prints, many telling unique stories about the culture and the maker.

The Javanese have used this technique for centuries, passing it down from generation to generation. Though it now has some mainstream usage in the fashion industry—brands like Zimmerman and Ulla Johnson have both incorporated the technique into their collections—in Indonesia, you will see these patterns used to make kemben, a wrap worn underneath a sheer long-sleeve shawl that is part of the kebaya dress, the national costume for women.

Ibu Linna is a twenty-nine-year-old craftswoman who has lived in the village her whole life. She is a fourth-generation batik maker who has fought hard to keep her traditions alive. She is married with a small child and makes her living at home working for a brand called SukkaCitta. Together with the designer, she makes beautiful garments, each featuring intricate patterns and splashes of color. She also teaches other women in her village the skills she has learned and helps them to make a living from their batik work.

"In my village, almost all women worked as batik craftsmen, in every house there must be a family who grouped together to make batik in the kitchen or in their yard," she told me in a long WhatsApp message that was filled with exclamation points and sweet smiley faces at the end of each sentence. We texted for a few days, only doing one small exchange at a time. The time difference between Indonesia and New York is about fourteen hours, and she was busy with her family and work. Phone calls were too difficult. She explained to me that despite being one of the oldest traditions in her area, batik craftsmen are few and far between. Once her village became a religious tourism site, the influx of people made other jobs like souvenir trading more lucrative. Many artisans moved away from the craft and on to better-paying roles. "Since then, about twenty years, batik craftsmen are increasingly rare. Only a few people survived," she said.

Traditional crafts in small villages are invaluable to preserving culture. They are connections, many of which are created through regalia and passed down through generations. It's the part of "fashion" that, to me, is the most special. Clothes keep us close to the past in ways that no other record can, they tell unspoken stories through textiles and colors and silhouettes. In batik, the makers repeat the same techniques as their great-grandmothers. Their hands are stained the same from dyes, they feel the same fabrics, get the same small blisters from holding the hot wax applicators. They will pass these skills down to their daughters and, in keeping the art alive, they keep the memory of their ancestors alive. As rural areas rapidly change due to political and religious upheaval, or in some cases tourism and industrialization, it's especially important that these traditions are kept by the people they belong to.

It's exactly why Ibu Linna was dedicated to keeping batik alive in Gesikharjo. After she finished school, her parents suggested that she try to find steady work in an office, so she did. Still, she knew she would return to the craft she loved so much. "In my heart, I always hoped to become a batik maker," she told me. Many of her peers still worked in textiles but had given up on batik because of the opportunities to use their coloring and sewing skills to make clothing for fashion brands.

Unlike the other garment workers that we've met, these women were contracted out by the workshops, who were contracted by the factories, which were contracted by a brand. Even though it's a common practice, it's far removed from the realm of any regulation set forth by any label, and because it can be extremely exploitative, it's not often talked about in the fashion industry. In small villages, where traditional jobs can no longer support people, this kind of work takes advantage of the local people's economic situations. Any paying work is crucial for survival, even when the wages are extremely low and the hours inhumane. There is often no choice. For her part, Ibu Linna kept her office job but made batik on the side until eventually she was introduced to a woman named Denica Flesch. Flesch wanted to work with the artisans in the neighborhood on her brand SukkaChitta. She is from Indonesia but left to study in Europe and become an economist. Like Ibu Linna, she felt strongly about continuing local artisan traditions, and wanted to find a way to do it while boosting the economy and supporting women.

Flesch traveled from village to village meeting women, seeking to understand the ways in which they maintained the culture and find out where they were struggling. "They took me in, and then shared their heritage with me, and it was beautiful," she recalled in a Zoom call with me one morning in August. "Still, I couldn't help but notice that they were struggling, all of them. They were stuck in a cycle of poverty, working crazy hours, being paid nothing. Their children already started abandoning the craft because the opportunities are simply elsewhere. The whole of Indonesia is basically rural if you get out of Jakarta." She reiterated that these women were bringing fabrics and dyes for random brands into their homes and working countless unregulated hours because they had no other options. They were still making very little money, just pennies per hour in some cases. But no one is talking about them when we talk about justice and ethics in fashion. "They are completely invisible," Flesch added.

Throughout this book, the picture I've painted of the underrepresented side of fashion looks similar. People, mostly women, working long hours in factories around the world. They are making much less than a living wage in sometimes dirty, unkempt facilities. Some are subject to abuse from managers, and not protected by the brands they're sewing clothes for. That's all true. But women whose artistic and cultural traditions are devalued by the same brands are a big part of this story, too. There are millions of workers in rural towns around the world making and finishing the clothing that ends up in our closets—and the information about them is scarce at best. As Flesch points out, they are often hidden—which becomes a problem that extends well beyond pay and into safety. Often the brands contracting these women are sending toxic chemicals used to dye clothing into their homes without informing them about the dangers of the materials. Some brands will use synthetic azo dyes, which contain nitrogen, and when these dyes break down they become carcinogenic. Flesch said some of the women she worked with had been unknowingly dumping synthetic dyes into the water where their children play, assuming it was safe when it wasn't.

Rebecca van Bergen, founder of the nonprofit organization Nest, explained to me that it's the exploitation of special skills and circumstance that have made the use of homeworking—when workers create products either in their homes or in small, often rural, workshops—by larger brands so much more sinister. Many of these women can't work in factories because they are simply too far out to travel to one, or they need the flexibility to raise children, or both. Brands like Amazon and Target, which have seen a demand for more homemade goods as consumer trends lean toward goods that feel more authentic, are using this system of workers already in place. So much of what we consume is mass-produced, and there appears to be a trend of authenticity and uniqueness. As much as people want to have something affordable, they also want something that feels like it has personality. Handmade items give the illusion of that.

While many advocates discourage homework because of the abuse that can occur, Van Bergen and designers like Flesch are hoping to change it so that it works for the women. "There was so much attention paid to factories, which is incredibly important. Because of that, so many companies had put together standards for regulating factories, but no one was looking at the hundreds of thousands of workers outside the factory," Van Buren said about starting Nest. The program seeks to pair artisan groups with brands as a way to make homework safer and fairer for the workers by giving them a voice in the process.

"There is a significant amount of home-based labor in our current supply chain. Whether it's stringing sea beads onto mass-market jewelry or embellishment on a pillow or a T-shirt—that work can be happening in someone's home." She also said that embracing terminology around the people who are working from home by calling them "handworkers" instead of homeworkers can be important step in contextualizing what they do. "Some of it is highly skilled artisanal labor and some of it is less so, but all of it is handwork, and so we really started embracing terminology." People who work from home creating and finishing garments are doing just as much, sometimes more, labor as those in other jobs, and yet they are completely devalued in both their pay and recognition.

As I began to understand more about this particular type of work, it became clear that the vulnerability and lack of action may have something to do with the fact that it is mostly women who are staying home to care for families and children and also taking on these subcontracted jobs. In 2020, there were an estimated 50 million women doing handwork in the fashion industry. Brands claim they can't regulate what they don't know, but how convenient is that?

Along with the deeply concerning fact that millions of women are being taken advantage of by an industry that uses female empowerment as a commodity, I found that there is a common theme in the way these garment workers, especially handworkers, are spoken about. Often, I read stories referring to them as the ones at the "bottom" of the industry. While it's true that they are erased from the narrative, "the bottom" feels inaccurate and patronizing. Handworkers are literally the hands of fashion, the people who touch our clothing more than any machine or even designer does. Looking at them as anything other than that perpetuates an idea that they are somehow worth less than any other person who keeps this industry churning.

It's the "girlboss" complex: we see fashion as a place where women are empowered, but only certain women. We prop up them up and put them on panels to talk about how women can make millions if they want to and take what's theirs. But we're living in a feminist dystopia if we clap for the girlbosses and then completely erase other women based on the type of work they are doing. Especially when it benefits the ones in the spotlight; the cognitive dissonance it takes to do that never ceases to amaze me.

As I sat down to write this chapter, I put on a shirt that was a gift from SukkaCitta and the women in Gesikharjo. Maybe that's cheesy, but unlike most of the clothing in my closet, I know exactly who made it and I wanted to honor them by feeling the weight of the fabric as I tried to tell their stories. It's a black tank top with colorful thin straps dyed in warm shades of yellow, maroon, and orange. It has beautiful stitching down the front that's so subtle you have to look closely to see the detail. I put it on because the hands that dyed and sewed and cut threads on this top are just as important as those of anyone else in the fashion industry, and the fact that they are so easily forgotten is the industry's biggest failure.

Inside the box that the tank top was sent in there was a small packet that had letters and pictures from the women in the village about what making clothing has been like for them over the years. "Every time I dyed fabrics, my chest would hurt from inhaling all those fumes. And my hands burned too," one woman shared, highlighting the serious impact that synthetic dyes sent from fast fashion brands had on her health. Also in the packet was a picture of Ibu Linna proudly holding up the batik she made, giving the camera a big contagious smile. "Just a few days before she passed, my grandmother gifted me one of her most beautiful batik fabrics and asked me to promise to continue her craft," her note reads. In fashion, we tend to look at the finished product. The models cascading down the runway. The beautiful dress hanging on the rack. We can so easily separate the person who made it from the item itself, and that allows the erasure of these women. To know that the top I'm wearing was created by a woman fulfilling her family legacy has so much more power than a flat garment I picked up randomly.

This rings especially true as I've seen a push for handmade items over the last several years grow rapidly. At a certain point around 2015 or 2016 there was a "makers" market in every small town and every open hipster space you could see. I had friends who curated some of these, picking vendors and decorating spaces so that everyone from college students to moms with three kids in strollers felt excited to walk through. There were DJs playing vinyl records, mixing the Smiths with Rihanna. At the outer edges of the space were craft beer and coffee stands, with tables blocking off the corners of the room. Both would have long lines, because each person who went up to order ended up talking about the intricacies of brewing either beverage.

Aisles in the room were filled with sellers who had just started their side business making handmade soaps or handmade cutting boards out of their garages. Then there would always be one or two jewelers touting their handmade earrings and necklaces, placed next to someone selling hand-dyed smocks. No one was looking at the makers in the same way we look at others around the world in the homeworking space. They were looked at as entrepreneurs with creative side hustles. We value that, we respect that.

At one of the markets, I learned that a designer for a major brand had been there: one of the jewelers told me that this person had walked over to their booth to check out their jewelry and see if they would be interested in selling it at their store. "They want to curate a handmade section in the SoHo shop," they told me. There was consumer interest in crafts made by one person in their home, and brands were tapping into it.

What I think we all neglected to realize was that craft wasn't some resurging thing and it wasn't some pushback on social media and technology that had sped up our lives in the decade prior. This kind of crafting and artisan work was just packaged a little differently. It was primarily white people in the United States making things and charging high (and appropriate) prices for their labor and materials. You very well could purchase a hand-beaded necklace for $8, it's just that we don't value that item enough to look at the hand that made it in her home somewhere on the other side of the world and pay her adequately for the work she's done.

On the designer side, there are certainly some who carefully source their embroidery and beading to help boost and revive rural communities. But there is an element of deceptive marketing that can come with these claims of handmade—one that adds another level of exploitation. Many designers aren't necessarily taking the care to intimately understand the needs of the women in certain regions. They simply say something is homemade in a certain area but fail to provide any further transparency. How much are the artisans being paid? What does that structure look like? How are you ensuring that the companies aren't bringing toxic chemicals into workers' homes and villages? How are their hours being monitored? It may seem like a lot, but just like we have to ask questions to avoid the greenwash, we should ask the same of seemingly ethical handmade companies as well.

Many of these designers get a lot of praise and attention when they are transparent about their materials and processes, which is ultimately a very good thing. It encourages other designers to rethink how they are hiring out their work, and where they could be putting resources. However, I have always felt that attention in the fashion industry is an addiction. I see it with influencers and editors. When that spotlight is on you, whether it's from Anna Wintour or some other hotly sought-after approver of all things fashion, it is warm and bright. It can also go away fast, so people will do whatever they can to stay in it. Sometimes that means sacrificing the very principles they founded their brand on.

With fast fashion, it's less about where we place the spotlight and more about how the secrecy and hiding benefit the bottom line. These brands are able to sidestep regulations because there is no appropriate auditing practice in place. But there needs to be. For the millions of workers who live in rural areas, this type of arrangement with employers is important for them to be able to remain in their hometowns with their families. They shouldn't be forced to leave to go into big-city factories when it's clear they can use their skills to work from home and build up communities domestically.

"I think that the challenge becomes how you monitor, how you provide educational resources, how you support, how you adapt and change and build, and so I sometimes think it's misplaced in that there's all these fears put on homework, when there's all of those same challenges in regulated factories," Van Bergen said. She also said that because of backlash against homeworking, brands will pull from their suppliers instead of trying to remediate. It doesn't necessarily seem like a solution when the women need the work and will likely have to take it regardless of whether it's safe or well paid. It would be more valuable for brands to work on formalizing what is created by handworkers so that we have more data and access to streamline it.

It's especially interesting when you consider how our attitudes toward working at home changed throughout the COVID-19 pandemic. In the early months, while the virus was spreading and testing was difficult to find, people were quitting jobs they once prided themselves on in order to find flexible work from home so that they could stay safe. This is not to say that any of us were making a connection between our new desires to build a home office and the people who have been working from home for centuries, but the newfound empathy could open doors to talk about what's been going on in the homes of women like Ibu Linna in Indonesia. When factory garment workers who were making PPE were getting sick and dying due to the close stations at their job, many of them switched to working at home. That should have indicated an incentive to legitimize this type of work and regulate it in a way that would help the workers make living wages.

"There's nothing good that can come out of what's already happened during the pandemic," Van Bergen said. "Millions of people have gotten sick and died but there is opportunity in recognizing the inequality around the world." If we can have multilateral conversations among the governments in Asia and South America as well as the brands who are working with factories who subcontract with no tracing or consequence for that, then perhaps we can start to protect the workers who have been ignored.

9

"It's Not That Serious"

New York Fashion Week in 2014 was one of the most memorable weeks of my entire career. At the time, I was a scrappy young reporter taking any fashion-adjacent gig I could find. I would take sick days from my day job filing papers at a textbook company and try to get into any show I could. I was getting paid so little per story from the outlets I was writing for that I lost money with the number of times I had to swipe onto the subway. Somehow, though, just being there was a dream come true. On one of those days, about halfway through the week—when I was riding both a high for getting to this point in my career and a low of two hours of sleep per night because of all the stories I was filing—I received an email from a beauty blog asking me to report on a show taking place in the Meatpacking District of Manhattan.

Fashion Week was changing drastically. Shows that had been in a central hub of Bryant Park or Lincoln Center had begun to splinter across the entirety of New York City at the whim of designers. Bloggers and influencers were now the ones to watch, and those of us reporting on the shows, especially ones without fancy titles at big magazines, were seated merely as a formality. I didn't mind the change, to be honest. Sure, running around was inconvenient, but was I really going to complain about being at the top of Rockefeller Center in Midtown and inside the gorgeous Kings Theatre in Brooklyn in the same week? (*No* is the answer you're looking for.) The catch, though, was that you'd always be late. And not in a cute, fashionably late way. Shows were scheduled one right after another, and you had to try to get to all of them, with traffic and subway schedules making it nearly impossible. As a result, the people producing and working at the shows all seemed miserable as they tried to make sure people got there and seats were filled.

I don't recall what brand this particular Meatpacking District show was for, because I never made it inside. By the time I arrived, there was a small group of very late editors waiting to go up in an elevator to see it. At the door there were two young PR assistants checking names before we were allowed to head up. The pair were clearly stressed out, flipping through pages of names and talking quietly but sternly into the tiny Bluetooth microphones attached to their heads.

"She's not here yet," I heard one of them mutter with a clenched jaw. As the rest of us waited patiently for them to let us in, the elevator behind the two women opened up. Out of it walked an older woman who I assumed was their boss. "What the fuck is going on here?" she asked much louder than I think she intended. She turned her back to the line and ripped the paper from the PR girl's hand. She started furiously flipping through the pages as she turned back to us and said, "Okay, let's go." She waved her hand toward the elevator curtly, never looking up from the paper.

The assistant, now left without her packet of names, looked to her left and to her right and then sort of stumbled to the elevator. As it opened, she turned back to her boss, who was now furiously crossing off names, and asked, "What floor?" referring to the runway show that was somewhere upstairs. This set the woman in charge off. She turned to her assistant and screamed, "Stop being such an idiot!" An objectively harsh command for someone seemingly doing nothing wrong. But if that wasn't horrifying enough, as she finished yelling at the assistant, she let out a breath and reached her hand into her pocket to pull out what looked like a credit card. She chucked the card at her assistant as hard as she could, hitting the young woman in the back of the head right as the doors jerked back as she held the door opened as it started to close.

As the assistant turned to face us, still holding the elevator door open, we could all see the embarrassment fill her face, redness burning up from her chin to her forehead. The manager knew what we'd just seen, but ignored it all and she went right back to her sheets of paper anyway.

The few of us standing in the hallway just looked at each other, appalled. We should have said something to that woman. We should have told the boss that her behavior was unacceptable, but we didn't. We just walked away from the show hoping that our protest would be enough to show them how gross that conduct was.

It was abusive—but at the same time it was the norm for fashion bosses at that time and something the younger crowd like me was used to. You simply can't say anything when you're treated like that because this is a dream job, and anyone can take it out from under you (and the whole industry makes sure you're aware of it). As we walked away, we hobbled down the cobblestone streets of the West Side toward the subway, my cheap high heels on the brink of collapse with every broken brick. One writer, who seemed to be around my age and position in the industry, turned to me and said in a quiet tone so that the others couldn't hear, "It's just fashion, it's not that serious."

In that moment her sentiment was applicable. Crossing

names off a list and sitting people at a fashion show is no reason to assault another person—that's absurd. But the phrase she used always stuck with me. I heard it all the time whenever something got a little too heated at work.

Fashion isn't that serious, so just take a breath, walk away, move through it. "We're not saving lives," some people often add. *Okay. Sure.* I think that if we looked at fashion as something that is actually quite serious, though, maybe we would look past the fashion shows and the department stores and the influencers and realize that fashion is so much bigger than what you or I can even comprehend. Especially when we recognize that fashion's workforce, from that PR assistant to the woman who made the clothes the late editors had to see so badly, has been an integral part of evolution in both the fashion industry and the world. It's not to say that what happened that day wasn't *just* fashion, it's that it *was* fashion at its most sincere. That behavior was indicative of the type of very real and very serious disrespect and abuse that has been tolerated throughout the industry for decades. Right in front of my eyes was a display of the industry's worst tendencies, the ones that prioritize hierarchy, ignore workers, and so much more in order to create an image of perfection.

Historically, it's been garment workers leading social change and saving lives. In the early twentieth century, women garment workers marched in the streets of Manhattan and demanded that conditions in the workplace change for everyone in the United States. And in the twenty-first century, garment workers stood on the frontlines of the pandemic and of social justice movements to fight for a better future.

In the beginning of 2020, when PPE shortages put the lives of thousands of doctors and nurses at risk, fashion labels around the world, including Louis Vuitton and Burberry, halted production and shifted their factories to making hospital gowns and masks. While the brands got praise and thanks, it was the people sewing and cutting the garments who were risking their safety to come into work and make the clothing. Most of the factories didn't even pay their workers for the canceled orders that had come in before the production switch, leaving them without pay and many of them sick. Still, they went in and ended the shortage that threatened the global healthcare system.

In Myanmar, garment workers were in the spotlight for this exact reason after several fast fashion brands making clothing in factories converted their productions to making masks. In a report by *Buzzfeed* in May 2020, five hundred workers in factories that made clothing for Zara claimed that they were fired when they asked for proper PPE before going into work. Inditex later refuted the claim, but provided no proof either way, and a spokesperson for the brand simply stated that they followed the protocols set forth by the government at that time. It was the brand's word against the workers, but at the end of the day hundreds of people were left scrambling for new jobs in the pandemic. But that was just the beginning of a year of turmoil for workers there.

On February 1, 2021, a military coup took over the democratically elected government in Myanmar. The military detained members of the National League for Democracy, cabinet ministers, chief ministers of several regions, opposition politicians, writers, and activists. As the *New York Times* explained the coup, the military took over the country, canceled flights, and turned off internet and telephone access in some cities. The outlet also reported that banks had been closed and people had to wait in long lines to access money from ATMs.[1] The reaction in the immediate aftermath was peaceful as protesters took to the streets to highlight their opposition. But on February 20, two protesters were killed by the military and things took a turn for the worse. By the middle of the following week, a general strike brought millions of people into the streets to fight back. On the front lines were garment workers, led by union leaders like Ma Moe Sandar Myint, an organizer with the Federation of General Workers Myanmar.

"On the morning of that day, I was in a meeting with union leaders, and we were very close to the place where the confrontations happened. The Tatmadaw [armed forces] started the crackdown after 12 PM. They used tear gas, sound bombs, and then real bullets. Many people were killed," she told *Jacobin* about the early days of the takeover.[2] She went on to explain that once the military declared martial law, the union workers changed their strategy from "strikes with thousands of workers on the roads to protests based at townships or wards, and to preparing defense systems."

Myanmar is big business for fashion, with $4.59 billion worth of exports coming from the country each year. As the protests were happening, garment factories reopened and workers had to go in despite the danger. This caught global attention when photos appeared in the international press showing garment workers holding up signs urging brands like H&M, Zara, and

Mango to stop placing orders in the country and allow them to continue to fight back against the coup. Initially the protest signs didn't prevent the brands from placing orders and workers had to risk their lives to keep coming in to make clothing. On March 14 of that year, nearly sixty garment workers were killed in the garment district of Hlaingthaya when the military went in with tanks, trapped people, and killed them.

After the massacre, Remake CEO Ayesha Barenblat and activist and author Elizabeth L. Cline hosted an emergency press conference over Zoom with workers in the area so that they could get their message across. Ko Aung, of the Federation of General Workers Myanmar (FGWM), told the group of about fifteen reporters what she was currently dealing with. "We sew for Mango, Zara, Primark. Mostly European brands," she explained through a translator from the union. "There has been a lot of union solidarity. Military has been shooting us with live ammunition. This has had a big impact on the factory zones, with many factories shutting down. Safety to get to work has been a big concern. We want international brands to push suppliers to stand with workers." She went on to add that workers had to flee to rural areas, but there is concern about starvation because of the lack of income. There is no good choice, she said. The workers needed the brands to step in and support their right to peacefully protest instead of forcing them into work, where they would be in harm's way.

By April, H&M had stopped placing orders, and carefully worded the announcement about the pause to say they were simply "watching" the situation. Many other brands continued on, business as usual. Eventually H&M started up again too. The brand said it was to "avoid the imminent risk of our suppliers having to close their factories which would inevitably result in unemployment for tens of thousands of garment workers." That wasn't untrue in the short term, but if people were dying to get to their job, did it really matter? The issue was deeper for the unions. Their leadership made it clear that even under democratic rule, there were major issues with wages and treatment—around 60 percent of workers in Myanmar are making less than $2 an hour.

"If there were rights violations before in factories, then under a military regime there is no question that things will be even worse for garment workers with low-wage jobs," Ma Moe Sandar Myint told the *New York Times*. "This is a fight I must take on. We can't accept this, even if it means risking arrest or death. It's for me, my family, my union colleagues and all the people of Myanmar." In the months after, workers continued to ask brands to stop business in the country until the dictatorship was removed, and each one of them chose profit over people once again.

So much of what I discovered and the notes I wrote down as I talked to dozens of people over the course of six months is that garment work, fashion work, style, clothing—all of it—is woven into politics. There are countless examples of the ways in which people have used their outfits to make statements about where they stand on something politically. Women in the United States Congress wore white, representing women's right to vote to protest Donald Trump on more than one occasion. In 2018, there were protests in Iran, where hijab is required for women. Some of the protesters, like Saba

Kord Afshari, took to the streets of Tehran and stood above crowds as they removed their hijabs from their heads. Afshari was later arrested and sentenced to ten years in prison for "inciting and facilitating corruption and prostitution."[3] In France, women had to protest for their right to wear hijab in public after the country outlawed them. They mobilized #PasToucheAMonHijab (#HandsOffMyHijab) in order to raise awareness of how rules policing what women wear in any way are misogynist and rooted in colonialism. What we put on our bodies, from seed to sew to closet, can be a radical symbol of something bigger. Sometimes a cute top is just a simple expression of self, for sure, but before it even got to you, that top was layered with the fight for equality and independence of people around the globe. Even it's a just a T-shirt, we have to understand the connections that piece of sewn cotton has to the rights of women on this planet, whether it's fighting against a dictatorship or fighting for the most basic human rights.

In Xinjiang, China, Uyghurs, the Muslim minority group in the country, have been subject to arbitrary mass detention of an estimated 1 to 1.8 million people. The U.S. State Department under both Donald Trump and Joe Biden labeled this forced assimilation a genocide. In July 2021 their report concluded, "the People's Republic of China is committing genocide and crimes against humanity against Uyghurs, who are predominantly Muslim, and members of other ethnic and religious minority groups in Xinjiang. The crimes against humanity include imprisonment, torture, enforced sterilization, and persecution." It was a damning report that seemingly slipped under the radar in the same way that so many of these stories have in the past, especially in fashion.[4]

Xinjiang is the largest producer of cotton in the world— much of it is farmed, treated, and manufactured by Uyghurs in forced labor camps.[5] Xinjiang cotton is so ubiquitous within the global supply chain that the likelihood that there is a forced labor–produced garment in your closet is extremely high. Jewher Ilham, a Uyghur, has been an advocate since her father was detained at the airport in China on his way to the United States in 2013. Ilham was with him at the time and was only allowed to leave because she was a teenager. Her father was an economist who is serving a life sentence for speaking out about the government. "My father was one of the very first people who got arrested when this all began," Ilham told me over a Zoom call from her friend's home in Indiana. It was during a point in the pandemic when online activism was having a real moment. People were trapped inside, on their phones, able to take the time to see injustice around the world. Ilham was looking to use that momentum to bring attention to her father's case. "He got arrested for his public advocacy for Uyghurs and speaking up for the Uyghur rights. He was a scholar, and all his speeches and his activism were mainly based on his research on the socioeconomic issues in the Uyghur region. He was proposing ideas and also criticizing the government for certain policies in the Uyghur region towards the Uyghur people, and the government didn't take it very well."

She went on to explain that he also created a website to disseminate this information because some social media platforms are banned. "The majority of people in China are receiving very censored and biased information which is released by the state-backed media CCTV," she explained. He feared that stereotypes about Uyghurs were being weaponized against them, creating more isolation of the people through the media, and he wanted to create a space where Han Chinese people and Uyghurs could "bond," through a chat function.

After getting shut down several times, her father was eventually arrested and sentenced to life in prison. Ilham explained that her cousin was also arrested simply for having a picture of her father on their phone, and seven of his students were also arrested. According to Ilham, no one knows where they are or how long they have been sentenced for. "The only reason that they released information of my father was because he was well known enough that he had the international community's attention. There was no way that the Chinese government could cover it up," she said sternly. In 2017, visitation was banned, and that was the last time Ilham spoke with her father. She also cannot communicate with her family for fear of retribution. The only way she can speak to her family is to have Han Chinese friends visit them and try to contact them through their devices. "We switch ten different platforms. Some of them get blocked, some of them get hacked, some of them stop working after a few days. We try not to communicate with each other too frequently, because that's only going to cause more damage to them than anything positive."

Despite the potential dangers of speaking out, Ilham told me that the best way she can help her father is to tell his story. Specifically, she wanted to appeal to the industries, like fashion, that have profited from the labor of exploited Uyghur people.

"We need to hit [the government] where it hurts," she explained. "That is why targeting corporations and using government sanctions to stop imports is a strategy that could work."

Roughly one in five cotton garments sold globally contain cotton or yarn from the Uyghur region—an incomprehensibly large amount of clothing is made in conditions that violate the ethical promises made by the brands you may be shopping from. "[Brands] have the resources to find out that information about where they are sourcing cotton. They have the ability to ask for disclosure from their suppliers. If they don't know, especially if we're talking about like a huge company, they're choosing not to know," Penelope Kyritsis, of the Worker Rights Consortium, said in that same call.

Ilham gave me an example of one worker who was part of the labor transfer program, bringing Uyghurs from their home in Xinjiang to the cities through an assimilation tactic used by the government. She explained that her mother, "a kind person with a big heart that doesn't want to get involved in politics," had met this woman one day on the streets of Beijing and saw that one of her hands was burnt. The woman told her that she had been transferred to the city to work in a Uyghur clothing factory, where she was injured. When her mother asked her if she wanted to leave, the woman said she couldn't unless someone became a guarantor for her—something that most people won't do because of the potential backlash. Despite the risks, Ilham's mother took her in as a housekeeper.

In 2021, the United States, under pressure from activists and human rights groups, banned imports of cotton from the region, forcing brands to make public choices about their supply chain in China. Activists put together a call-out for brands to sign to say they would not support the forced labor of Uyghurs, but it was tricky. Nike, Adidas, and Burberry spoke out about sourcing in the region, all putting out statements about their concerns. It became complicated once Chinese state television began calling for boycotts of the brands because of the positions they had taken. "For enterprises that touch the bottom line of our country, the response is very clear: don't buy!" one tweet from China Central Television read. Another tweet showed lawmaker Regina Ip Lau Suk Yee staring at three Burberry scarves on her couch with the caption, "I will stop buying or using Burberry products until Burberry has retracted or apologized for its unfounded allegations against Xinjiang."

Nike's sales were impacted and fell almost 59 percent that year globally. It was a risk that other brands sourcing from the region refused to take. H&M initially condemned the forced labor in the area publicly, but backtracked by deleting their statement and reiterating their commitment to their Chinese customers. This dilemma, to me, illustrates the fashion industry's moral conundrum better than anything else we have examined. Activists and governments are not mincing words when it comes to what is happening to the Uyghur people in China, calling Chinese actions genocide. And yet brands are struggling to choose between losing out on a huge market and being a part of the push to end the detainment camps in the country. How much clearer can the choice be?

Activism, especially through worker-led movements, can and does work. In Bangladesh, the second-largest exporter of garments after China, unions worked tirelessly to rewrite the

Bangladesh Accord that was put in place following the Rana Plaza disaster that killed thousands of garment workers. The new agreement, called the International Accord for Health and Safety in the Textile and Garment Industry, was signed by two hundred brands and went into effect on September 1, 2021. The replacement agreement is legally binding and places new oversight on training, inspection, and safety in factories in the area. It's a big change that will give workers a voice when brands behave badly in the area and ensure that the people who died in 2013 will not have done so in vain.

In California, workers who have fought for decades, through the protests in the 1990s and beyond, finally had their voices heard. Santa, Maria, and Lorena, the three Los Angeles–based garment workers who spoke to me about their experience with abuse in fashion, all put their jobs at risk to talk about their inadequate pay as they fought for a bill called SB-62 to pass in the California state legislature. In September 2021, after years of working to end sweatshops in the United States, countless protests, and calls with reporters, Governor Gavin Newsom signed the bill into law, effectively ending any loopholes that allowed brands to pay workers less than the minimum wage. This bill made brands legally accountable for their suppliers who pay workers per piece, or less than minimum wage.

Two days later, standing in front of the fashion trade show in downtown Los Angeles carrying signs that said, "Make LA Sweatshop Free," a large crowd of garment workers and their supporters shouted, "Cuando luchamos, ganamos!" (When we fight, we win!). The Garment Worker Center's director, Marissa Nuncio, spoke first, standing in front of the crowd, emotional as she began. "I'm usually not nervous, but I'm so excited and still in shock," she told the excited group that stood in front of her. Before she introduced other workers and supporters to speak, she said a few brief words that I felt were so moving and poignant, you should read them in full:

> Why are we here today? Because as of this Monday SB-62 is the law. Workers' demands to end the piece rate system and their demands to hold the fashion industry responsible for wage theft became law. [Their demands created] a more level playing field for those companies working hard to run an honest business because [doing so] is now required by law. We're here at this fashion trade center during a trade show to speak to the industry, we're here as a symbol of what workers and our supporters have been fighting for. Workers made the determined and brave decision to organize and demand real tangible structural change within the garment industry. They exposed the exploitative core of this industry and demanded that power shift away from the multimillion-dollar fashion brands' control towards workers. Towards justice in the workplace.

It's so easy to feel pessimistic about everything in this industry, especially as you learn just how deep the issues are, and how the fashion dystopia is real. When fast fashion expanded, people said, "Slow down—we will hurt people if we have to keep up with this pace." Nothing slowed down and conditions got worse. When seasons ramped up, people said, "Do less, or our landfills will overflow." The seasons have only gotten faster and the landfills continue to fill. We're so far from where we need to be, to the point where feeling like "it's all just going to get worse" is normal. The wins, though: that's where the will to keep pushing for change comes from. They clear the fog so that we can see that an equitable future is possible.

10

These Stories Are Real

As I was finishing this book, I quit my full-time job as a fashion editor. It wasn't the first time I'd quit a job in magazines, and who knows, maybe it won't be the last. Each time I pulled away from having a title in this industry it was like ripping off a sweater that was already kind of itchy but that I'd gotten so used to wearing that I felt naked without it. I had an identity crisis of sorts. When I left *Teen Vogue* in 2018 it felt like a rug had been quickly pulled out from under me, leaving me embarrassed and bruised. It was the first time I realized how much power came with the title I had and, subsequently, the false sense of importance I got from having it.

The second it was gone, people who I thought were my friends barely cared to say hello. It hurt. It made me feel like my role had nothing to do with talent or a keen eye, but simply luck and a willingness to promote brands in favor of clicks. Despite the fact that I was still a writer, when brands could no longer filter their flashy campaigns and celebrity marketing initiatives through me, my opinion was suddenly unnecessary. It was my own fault for thinking otherwise; the industry showed itself to me at every door I knocked on. Being exclusionary is how it stays relevant. Speak up about what you don't like and forget about any sense of community you thought you had. Those connections were all there to feed off you.

When I left *InStyle* it was less dramatic. The pandemic was still the top story, and my fashion writing was taking a back seat to the buzzy celebrity stories my job required. It wasn't that I didn't see the value in this kind of coverage, it was that it had become draining. In the summer of 2021, I was presented with an opportunity to write a newsletter about fashion in the way I wanted to. So, I left. I was happy with the decision and excited to be out of the constant flow of trend cycles and celebrity news. Still, a sense of identity loss lurked around me. Who was I without the title of "editor" at a magazine? It was the job I'd dreamed of my whole life.

Something that struck me was how out of the loop I felt, almost instantly. It's not a secret that fashion coverage can sometimes be defined by a handshake and a good relationship between an influencer or editor and a brand. But the second that relationship changes out of their favor, most brands don't want anything to do with you.

That's not to say that fashion editors don't love the brands we're writing about or that we don't believe in them. Often, we do. Or at least, I do. But it would be a straight-up lie if I didn't admit that the way I get to know a lot of brands is through the PR people who work there, or the founders and CEOs. They take us out to dinner and bring us on cool experiences that I would never be able to do on my own. I don't mean this flippantly; it's a privilege beyond my own comprehension sometimes. It only happened, though, because of the perceived value I had at the time. I was one of just a few doors into coverage they deemed vital to the growth of the brand. It makes sense, of course. And I wouldn't expect them to spend money on someone who couldn't bring them that. But what this experience did for me was highlight the power that the established fashion industry has on the entire ecosystem.

Keeping secrets about what happens behind the curtain is part of the whole mystique of fashion media, and that's why what I'm about to tell you is important. The majority of magazines have been in a transition for the last decade, if they even made it to the present (rest in peace to so many glossy pages I loved before). Part of that transition has been dealing with declining revenue, and so it's understandable that the magazines are at the mercy of advertisers. While I was given some freedom to cover stories about sweatshops or discrimination, I was also made to take down stories that reflected poorly on a brand that was paying to have their clothing in the magazine. It's not a stretch for me to say that the brand's bad behavior was covered up by me and by the decision-makers who decided to pull a piece, saying it was "unfair" when really it was just unfavorable.

Outside of advertising, there is affiliate shopping. I have written dozens of stories with affiliate arrangements for holidays and events. Basically, the magazine gets a certain negotiated percentage of whatever sells from the story that we write. It's not technically sponsored, and the stories will disclose that it is affiliate, but there is absolutely incentive to cover. Amazon fashion, for example, gives one of the best rates out there, and most magazines have full editorial plans around Prime Day and Black Friday. A story featuring "The Best Black Boots on Amazon" is serviceable for readers who are googling that, sure, but it's also contributing to consumption without much scrutiny aside from an edit of what a tastemaker thinks is cool. The conundrum is that it's a huge revenue stream for fashion media and it's become the focus.

I don't have a quick answer to the question of how to change the business model, but I do think it's important as a fashion editor to acknowledge the role I have played in this. I'm not suggesting that anyone quit their job like I did, but recognizing the power dynamics is the first step in changing this industry for the better. Exposing the problems in fashion by saying them out loud, writing about them, posting about them on social media, and acknowledging our part in perpetuating them is the key to making a change.

Why should I get flown around the country and wined and dined by a brand that can't even give their workers the respect of a living wage? Why is it that their priority is to make me comfortable while their factories are in chaos? It's because the story that I tell as a fashion editor is incredibly important to their overall brand identity. The real story doesn't matter as long as you, the reader, think that a fashion editor, the taste-maker of style, thinks they are cool.

It pains me to say it, but so much of this industry, including the jobs that I dreamed about having for so long, is bullshit. When I was in high school, I had a cover of *Teen Vogue* taped to the inside of my locker so that every day I remembered exactly what I wanted to do with my life. It's all I ever wanted and that's why I want it to be better—I didn't dream of pushing people toward clothing on Amazon that I wouldn't even buy myself because the magazine gets 3 percent of the sale. It's also why I want to empower you to make choices that feel good and to arm yourself with knowledge about how this whole thing works.

Practically speaking, it's a difficult situation to navigate. I could tell you to shop less, and I really hope you do. I hope you love your clothes; cherish the way they make you feel when you wear them and buy more only when you really need to. But as someone who loves clothing more than is probably healthy, I know that it's not completely realistic to ask the majority of the population to just stop buying new clothing. Also, the conversation around shopping less is not just about fashion— it's universal. Overconsumption has led to landfills piling up, impacting local water supplies and economies. We know this.

The reason we need brands involved in this change is because without them millions of workers will lose their jobs and the ones that remain will still be unsafe and unregulated.

Sandra Capponi, the co-founder of Good On You, a website that rates brands based on sustainability and ethics, explained why we need to get brands involved in a way that was very simple. Her site is unique in that it recognizes that people ulti- mately want to buy the right thing, but there is no system in place to help them choose what that might be. On the web- site you can plug in a brand's name and they give them a rat- ing based on the brand's work around the environment and their supply chain transparency. She said that brands need to take accountability for their business practices by upholding contracts and paying suppliers, but more than that they need to actively address the role they play in the problem and not kick it down to factories. "Brands should address the power imbalance with suppliers that allows them to exploit vulner- able populations and squeeze factories whenever they're in trouble, without any care for actions which can destroy peo- ple's livelihoods," she explained. "Brands need to find ways to support their suppliers and empower their workers, especially in times of crisis, and to strive for continuous improvement and equality."

We can't just trust brands to make changes on their own, of course. They have proven for decades that they are willing to say one thing and do another. We can put public pressure on them to adhere to standards set forth by organizations like Fair Trade or the Fair Wear Foundation. We can make sure that we are researching just a little bit before we click "buy." If we don't find what we want—we can ask the brands why they haven't made commitments.

There is no award for purity in your choices here. Fashion is a business built on consumption, and that consumption employs millions. Even after I spent months researching and writing about all of the terrible ways in which our clothing is made, I have had to grapple with the fact that it's not just going to stop, and these brands aren't going away. And, in a lot of ways, I don't want them to. They have the ability to make changes that can improve the livelihoods of the people who work for them, and we can all be a part of it.

To understand more about how change can happen, I spoke with Shivam Punjya. He is a designer who owns part of his own factories in India, which make accessories for his brand Behno. He started in apparel, but moved into classic leather handbags, made from naturally dyed leathers. Punjya grew up in Northern California and is of Southeast Asian descent, but he said it's important to be aware that he is an outsider in the places where his clothing is made. He can't understand the specific needs of his garment workers because they are different in each region of each country. That's why he suggests worker-led factories as a way of the future—meaning elevating seamstresses and taggers into positions where they are in charge of structuring the work environment. Just like the changes that we saw in California recently or in New York City after the Triangle Shirtwaist Factory fire, the most effective changes come when we the customer or the fashion-lover put the workers' needs first. And in turn, we push the brands to listen to them and work with them.

For Punjya, this doesn't just mean opening up his own place, it means working within the system to empower workers and change what's already happening. "Part of the movement requires us to find factories that are awful and working with them to turn them around because they start employing people. They started giving livelihood and it's how do we work within the system and improve it, rather than topple it? Because I also believe in double agency. I think that to make change, you have to work within existing systems."

Punjya gave me an example of one factory he was working with in Bangalore, in southern India. The factory, he explained, didn't have resources available to get clean water to the workers, so they had to bring their own. Punjya worked with them to get a portable water pump. Another factory was so cramped that there was no walking space in between machines. It would have been a huge problem if there were ever an emergency and people needed to be evacuated. In that case, they had to remove some machines—which can impact the amount of money they make. Punjya and his partners worked with the factory to adjust pricing to make up for the potential loss. "Very small things sometimes," he said. "But things that are so important at a day-to-day level that I think folks like me just take [them] for granted having worked in the U.S."

Of course, not all factories are willing to work with brands like Behno that will push back against wage theft and poor conditions. And until the bigger brands start doing the same, it won't have a huge impact. Either the factory has to be a willing participant in safety for the workers or there has to be enforcement from across the board; from huge corporations like H&M down to small independent designers. "They think that I'm coming in, trying to ruin their business model. And I think I'm voicing it, but I have to stand my ground. Like I think we want to work with folks like that but sometimes if we're not met with a collaborative ear, there's not much more I can do except say we won't work with you."

Behno is a small brand, and it can certainly have an impact, but it's simply not operating at the same scale as larger fashion brands. If brands worked closely with unions and worker-led coalitions within the factories instead of doing everything in their power to not only discourage organization but actively work against the policies they agreed to, we could see major changes for women around the world.

It's proof that the battle is uphill, and the solutions are not as linear as I'd hope. They lead you down paths with no destination, or dead ends with large brick walls that you can't see over. But I know the paths toward a better fashion industry are there, I know that workers will continue to fight for themselves, and that everyone buying clothing will continue to pay closer attention. I also know that the systems that have allowed the fashion industry to consistently turn its back on workers will get dismantled if we work at it.

There is power in naming the problem and pushing for those creating the narratives in fashion to do the same. There are people making the decisions that continue abusing workers. In fashion, holding the brands' founders accountable for these actions instead of putting them on a pedestal is a necessary step. When you search for Richard Saghian, the founder and CEO of Fashion Nova, one of the first articles that comes up calls him "enigmatic" and a "genius." Meanwhile, that genius business model is upheld by the women we heard from earlier who are making less than minimum wage. An article about billionaire H&M heir and now CEO Karl-Johan Erling Göran Persson calls him a "sustainability leader" and a "champion" of changing wage problems in the supply chain. Are those descriptors totally accurate, or are they a product of great public relations? He may very well be a champion of these issues and be actively working to change them, but until we actually see it, why is the story about him and what he *wants* to do, instead of an examination of why it hasn't been done yet?

At its core, fashion is about community and craft, and yet we've let these big corporations come in and steal that. Trends are perpetuated by influencers and social media's constant highlight reel. Fast fashion gives us that feeling of belonging in an instant. It warps our idea of connection by making us feel like we belong only if we buy into the same thing. What would happen if we stepped back and refused to allow them to have so much control?

In my neighborhood, there is a store that sells men's clothing. It's not a place that I shop for myself, but sometimes I'll go inside and look for someone else. The store prides itself on made-in-the-USA clothing, "stuff our grandfathers would be proud of" kind of thing. It leans heavy on machismo in its décor, but otherwise it's just basics. What struck me about it, however, was that as I walked in one day during the week I was finishing this book, I realized just how local it felt. Not all of the clothing was made in New York City—some came from Portland, Oregon. Still, the owner appeared to have curated it exactly to what felt right for the block it sat on. It was a little grungy, a little too Americana, but still classic and high quality. The type of clothing you'll hang on to for a lifetime and keep bringing back to that very store for a new hem or a stitch of repair. It didn't follow any trends, it just was what it was. I recognize that price is a barrier here, and some of the pieces I ran my hands over to glance at the tag were not exactly affordable. But they were clothes you could really love, and it struck me that sometimes that's what these big fashion corporations take from us. They take the love out of clothing. They take the love out of reading a story about a garment or a designer. And importantly, they take the love out of making clothing.

In the same way, as a journalist I wasn't always getting to write the pieces about the designers and the stylists that made me love clothes. The people who get to do that full time are few and far between. Corporate money and greed have corrupted the entire ecosystem, making it so that the brands get to do whatever they want, and we are always a few steps behind chasing them.

Making batik in Indonesia should be about craft and history, but instead it's become something that's toxic to the people who are doing it, and only being paid pennies for their carefully honed skill. Owning a piece of that should be like owning a piece of art, but instead it's something that we can add to a cart on a whim and throw away to never think about again.

We should be able to talk about these seamstresses and dyers knowing that their work is valued, and they are being paid. We can't do any of that.

And unlike me, most of the people who work in factories can't just leave their jobs. Garment work is the way millions of people make a living, and in many places it's one of the best jobs you can find. Change is not as simple as just shutting it all down. So, if we can't stop making something that makes up 2 percent of the world's gross domestic product, what do we do?

The answer isn't as simple as buying fewer new products, and switching to secondhand clothing like the narrative on social media often suggests. It's a good start, but as that grows, we're only going to see more fast fashion in different resale apps, something that is already happening. The answer is also not about pointing the finger at each other. When we do that, the biggest problem starters can sit back and watch us fight while they continue to make too much and pay too little.

The change will come from wiping away a bit of the shine and truly seeing the role people in the industry play. I love the glamour of a fashion show, but I no longer want it obscuring the real story of fashion. We need to see the workers of the fashion industry as the whole people that they are and, just like when you eat a meal at a restaurant knowing someone took the time to prepare it, and made it special for you, we should do the same with every piece of clothing that we own.

I come back to something that worker advocate Santa Puac said as we sat inside the Garment Worker Center that summer afternoon last year.

"Our stories are real," she proclaimed as she sat forward in her chair, leaning her arms on the table in front of her. At the time, I thought, "Of course they are," not realizing that this is the crux of the problem. Not that people think they aren't real, but rather that they'd prefer them not to be heard. It's more comfortable that way, and the brands take advantage of it.

So, it's important to recognize that the stories that you read are very real and deserving of your attention. The harassment, the poverty, the exploitation, and the pain inflicted upon people just trying to make a living through skilled work is real and we need to listen to them tell us what they are going through. And when they explain what they think is the right way to fix the problem, whether it's through worker-organized bill creation in partnership with government officials like SB-62, or unions making legally binding agreements with brands, we need to support them in those efforts in the way that they feel is most useful for them moving forward.

Often, brands are not taking the time to understand the unique needs of the factory workers in their supply chains—and employ someone who speaks the local languages and has an understanding of the region. Punjya explained that his brand has to prioritize different needs because, for example, "in the south of India, there's a lot more women that work in factories versus in the north of India it's a lot more male dominated." He went on to say that while the standards are the same, in one area he may need to focus more on gender-based discrimination that workers are speaking up about and in another it may be about wages or equipment safety.

Denica Flesch, in Indonesia, echoed Punjya's sentiment for all brands, even the ones that are trying to do the "right thing." "The language is really important; if you don't speak the same language it's very difficult to understand what the problems are. Foreigners may come with good intentions, but then because of the language barrier they're not able to really cross-check standards with the people they are supposed to be helping." It's important that designers are not taking a colonial approach by placing standards that they perceive as necessary instead of prioritizing the workers by putting their language and comfort first.

The fashion industry is not going to change overnight. We have a long, tumultuous road ahead that will likely serve little justice to those who have already been hurt. We can't only focus on how we got here, and how we all became part of this system. We have to focus on what's ahead. Just as I finished writing this book, a bill was written by Senator Kirsten Gillibrand's office that would take the principles of SB-62 and make them federal. It's called the FABRIC (Fashioning Accountability and Building Real Institutional Change) Act and, if passed, it could give tax incentives for brands to manufacturer in the United States. It would also give major grants to designers who want to make their factories safer for workers, and it would create a reporting structure for workers who have had their rights violated. Importantly, this could have happened at any time. There was nothing saying we couldn't make laws and incentives to make the U.S. garment industry bigger and better. It's happening only because workers refused to be silenced and people chose to support them. Counting on changes to individual consumer behavior alone will not shift this industry in the right direction but, with these bills, we can do something tangible anywhere in the United States. We can ask our representatives to support these laws, we can rally, and we can uplift the voices of the worker. Finally, people are listening and we cannot stop talking.

We also need to stop thinking about fashion as something that is a frivolous addition to life. Those ideas are rooted in sexist ideology about women's work and women's interests. Clothing is powerful for us as individuals and on a global scale for the millions of people who depend on it for their livelihoods and their culture. The lesson is not that we have to give up fashion entirely. In fact, it's quite the opposite. As people who wear and love fashion, we have to become better consumers and activists for a just industry. Before purchasing from any brand, look to see the commitments they've made. If they aren't listed anywhere that's easily accessible for you, then they probably haven't made them. And if that's the case, go a step further and ask them why they've chosen not to. When you do find brands that align with your values, hold them to the promises they make. Look for actions, not just words. This would include data about where their materials are coming from and testimonials from their workers. And most important, support legislation that holds brands accountable.

In the weeks after I spoke to Santa, she got a new job. She is now a worker advocate fighting to make sure that no worker in Los Angeles has the same experience she did. Her three adorable children, the youngest only one year old, will now live in a city that is at the forefront of change in the fashion industry because she told her story despite the consequences she could face—and will now fight to make sure it stays that way.

If listening to workers like Santa isn't a road map for how we change fashion, I don't know what is.

Acknowledgments

First, I would like to thank every person who was interviewed for this book. I'm so grateful for your time and your stories, especially under the circumstances with the pandemic. Most important, I want to thank Santa, Maria, Lorena, Ibu Linna, and Elba for standing up for workers, and making it possible for others to be seen and heard. And thank you to every garment worker, the millions of you around the world, because without you there is no fashion industry. I also want to express my gratitude toward the Garment Worker Center, specifically Marissa and Liz, for coordinating so many interviews. Thank you to the designers, Mara and Shivam, for your willingness to speak on all parts of your business, the good and the bad, so that we can better understand why these issues are so pervasive. Thank you, Madison and La'Shaunae, for bravely speaking up about your experiences, and continuing to make space for others to do the same. And to the activists and scholars,

Sel, Victor, Julie, Denica, Jewher, and Rebecca: thank you for unapologetically sharing your work and passion so we can all learn how to make change together.

I am deeply grateful for the people without whom this book would not exist. To my editor Rachel Vega DeCesario, whose patience and passion is on every page. To my agent Nicki Richesin, who saw the importance in this topic from the very beginning and encouraged me every step of the way. Also thank you to Michelle Del Rey, who transcribed and translated the interviews throughout the book.

Thank you to my mother Denise for being my biggest cheerleader, and advocate. To my father Jim for working so hard, showing me the dignity in all labor. To my sisters, Angelina and Andrea, I'm grateful to have been raised by two women who are unapologetically themselves and who have always been there for me even though I am the obnoxious baby sister. Thank you to my nieces and nephews, Molly, Sawyer, Abigail, Eliza, and Stas, for being a constant reminder of the good in the world.

I am grateful for the incredible women who make me, Kate, Nina, Lauren, Isabelle, Linsey, Tyler, and Ali. Thank you for being there every single second of this process, always just one text away. Thank you also to the ones I have met along the way while working in this industry, Peyton, Leah, Kim, Callia, Michaela, Brittney, Claire, Gabe, Alli, Isabel. Especially to Jessica, the person to whom I owe my entire career, this book would not be possible without your encouragement to tell the truth about this industry.

And lastly to my loving husband, Michael, whose support knows no bounds. Thank you for everything.

Notes

1: New Arrivals

1. Tara John, "How the US and Rwanda Have Fallen Out over Second-Hand Clothes," BBC, May 28, 2018.

2. Abigail Beall, "Why Clothes Are So Hard to Recycle," BBC, July 12, 2020.

3. James Laver, *Costume and Fashion: A Concise History* (London: Thames & Hudson, 1969).

4. Salman Rushdie, *The Wizard of Oz* (London: Bloomsbury Publishing, 2012).

5. Stephen Burgen, "Fashion Chain Zara Helps Inditex Lift First Quarter Profits by 30%," *The Guardian*, August 17, 2012.

6. ThredUP and GlobalData, *ThredUP 2021 Resale Report*, thredup.com /resale.

2: Made in America

1. Susan Shillinglaw, "75 Years After 'The Grapes of Wrath,' We Need Ma Joad in the White House," *Washington Post*, April 18, 2014.

2. Erin Blakemore, "20th-Century Slavery Was Hiding in Plain

Sight," *Smithsonian Magazine*, July 31, 2020, www.smithsonianmag.com/smithsonian-institution/20th-century-slavery-california-sweatshop-was-hiding-plain-sight-180975441.

3. Richard Appelbaum and Edna Bonacich, *Behind the Label: Inequality in the Los Angeles Apparel Industry* (Berkeley: University of California Press, 2000).

4. Steven Greenhouse, "Sweatshop Raids Cast Doubt on an Effort by Garment Makers to Police the Factories," *New York Times*, July 18, 1997.

5. Richard Harrington, "Rage Before Beauty," *Washington Post*, November 21, 1999.

3: Where Was Fashion's #MeToo?

1. Booth Moore, "Harvey Weinstein Puts Wife's Marchesa Fashion Brand in Tough Spot," *Hollywood Reporter*, October 9, 2017, www.hollywoodreporter.com/movies/movie-news/harvey-weinstein-puts-marchesa-fashion-brand-tough-spot-1046926.

2. Annie Kelly, "Worker at H&M Supply Factory Was Killed After Months of Harassment, Claims Family," *The Guardian*, February 1, 2021.

3. Prajwal Bhat, "B'luru Garment Workers Accuse Manager of Sexually Harassing Colleague, Case Booked," *The News Minute*, March 16, 2019, www.thenewsminute.com/article/b-luru-garment-workers-accuse-manager-sexually-harassing-colleague-case-booked-98410.

4. Louise Donovan and Refiloe Makhaba Nkune, "Exclusive: Workers in Factory That Makes Kate Hudson's Fabletics Activewear Allege Rampant Sexual and Physical Abuse," *Time*, May 5, 2021 (updated June 10, 2021), time.com/5959197/fabletics-factory-abuse-allegations.

4: The Illusion of Choice

1. Becky Johnson, "How Workers in Leicester's Textile Industry Are Still Being Exploited," *Sky News*, July 30, 2021, news.sky.com/story/how-workers-in-leicesters-textile-industry-are-still-being-exploited-12364671.

5: Influenced

1. Sydney H. Schanberg, "Six Cents an Hour," *Life*, March 28, 1996.

2. Ballinger, Jeffrey. "The New Free-Trade Heel." Harper's, August 1992. http://archive.harpers.org/1992/08/pdf/HarpersMagazine-1992-08-0000971

3. Simon Zadek, "The Path to Corporate Responsibility," *Harvard Business Review*, December 2004, hbr.org/2004/12/the-path-to-corporate-responsibility.

4. Ira Berkow, "Sports of the Times; Jordan's Bunker View on Sneaker Factories," *New York Times*, July 12, 1996.

5. Nike, *1998 Annual Report*, s1.q4cdn.com/806093406/files/doc_financials/1998/man_dis_any.html.

6. Vicky Xiuzhong Xu and James Leibold, "Your Nikes Might Be Made from Forced Labor. Here's Why," *Washington Post*, March 17, 2020.

6: The Secret Behind the Logo

1. Roberto Saviano, *Gomorrah: Italy's Other Mafia* (New York: Farrar, Straus and Giroux, 2006).

2. The United States Attorney's Office Eastern District of New York, "Four Defendants Arrested in Multimillion-Dollar Counterfeit Goods Trafficking Scheme," August 12, 2021, www.justice.gov/usao-edny/pr/four-defendants-arrested-multimillion-dollar-counterfeit-goods-trafficking-scheme.

3. David Marchese, "Dapper Dan on Creating Style, Logomania and Working with Gucci," *New York Times*, July 1, 2019.

4. Rob Haskell, "Can Gisele Save the Planet?" *Vogue*, June 14, 2018, www.vogue.com/article/gisele-bundchen-vogue-cover-july-2018-issue.

7: Green Is the New Black

1. H&M, *H&M Conscious Actions Highlights 2012*, about.hm.com/content/dam/hm/about/documents/en/CSR/reports/Conscious%20Actions%20Highlights%202012_en.pdf.

2. Lucy Siegle, "Is H&M the New Home of Ethical Fashion?" *The Guardian*, April 7, 2012.

3. Elizabeth Patton and Sapna Maheshwari, "H&M's Different Kind of Clickbait," *New York Times*, December 18, 2019.

9: "It's Not That Serious"

1. Russell Goldman, "Myanmar's Coup, Explained," *New York Times*, February 1, 2021.

2. Michael Haack and Nadi Hlaing, "In the Face of Massacres, Workers

in Myanmar Are Still Fighting the Coup," *Jacobin*, April 13, 2021, www
.jacobinmag.com/2021/04/myanmar-military-coup-massacre-workers
-hlaing-tharyar.

3. Center for Human Rights in Iran, "Mother of Jailed Anti-Compulsory
Hijab Activist Calls for Legal Reform," June 5, 2020, iranhumanrights.org
/2020/06/mother-of-jailed-anti-compulsory-hijab-activist-calls-for-legal
-reform.

4. Human Rights Watch, "'Break Their Lineage, Break Their Roots':
China's Crimes Against Humanity Targeting Uyghurs and Other Turkic
Muslims," April 19, 2021, www.hrw.org/report/2021/04/19/break-their
-lineage-break-their-roots/chinas-crimes-against-humanity-targeting.

5. Helen Davidson, "Xinjiang: More Than Half a Million Forced to Pick
Cotton, Report Suggests," *The Guardian*, December 15, 2020.

About the Author

A former senior news editor at *InStyle* and fashion news editor at *Teen Vogue*, **Alyssa Hardy** is the publisher of "This Stuff," a twice-weekly fashion newsletter. Her work has been featured in *Vogue*, *NYLON*, *Refinery29*, *Fashionista*, and elsewhere. She lives in New York City.

Publishing in the Public Interest

Thank you for reading this book published by The New Press. The New Press is a nonprofit, public interest publisher. New Press books and authors play a crucial role in sparking conversations about the key political and social issues of our day.

We hope you enjoyed this book and that you will stay in touch with The New Press. Here are a few ways to stay up to date with our books, events, and the issues we cover:

- Sign up at www.thenewpress.com/subscribe to receive updates on New Press authors and issues and to be notified about local events
- Facebook: www.facebook.com/newpressbooks
- Twitter: www.twitter.com/thenewpress
- Instagram: www.instagram.com/thenewpress

Please consider buying New Press books for yourself; for friends and family; or to donate to schools, libraries, community centers, prison libraries, and other organizations involved with the issues our authors write about.

The New Press is a 501(c)(3) nonprofit organization. You can also support our work with a tax-deductible gift by visiting www.thenewpress.com/donate.